THE EVACUATION
DIARY OF
HATSUYE EGAMI

THE EVACUATION DIARY OF HATSUYE EGAMI

edited and with an introduction by
Claire Gorfinkel

Intentional Productions
Pasadena, CA 1995

Published by Intentional Productions, P.O. Box 94814, Pasadena, CA 91109

Photographs, including cover ©Lucile Fessenden Dandelet, 1942
Drawings by Shigeko Elizabeth Ozawa
Map by George Matsuura
Book design by Anne Richardson-Daniel

Library of Congress number 95-079820

ISBN 0-9648042-1-2

DEDICATION

This publication is dedicated
to those whose actions
opposed racism and injustice in 1942,
those who continue to stand
in solidarity with the oppressed today,
and all who, like Mrs. Egami
strive for "higher planes of endeavor."

ABOUT THE ART WORK

The photographs (front and back cover, and pages 13 and 16) were taken in May 1942 by Lucile Fessenden Dandelet who was living in Pasadena after having graduated from Wellesley College. Shocked and horrified by the injustices she observed, Lucile saw her camera as a way to stop them. She currently continues to do professional photography from her home in San Anselmo, California.

The drawings (pages 27, 30, 61, 65 and 74) were made at Tulare Assembly Center in July and August 1942 by Shigeko Elizabeth Ozawa. She was a young mother who had studied at Pasadena City College, when she was interned at Tulare. She currently tends her family and her beautiful garden in Pasadena.

The map (pages 50 and 51) was drawn at Tulare Assembly Center in August 1942 by George Matsuura. George had graduated from the University of California before being interned. After the war George became a commercial artist in Illinois, where he now lives.

Intentional Productions
P.O. Box 94814 • Pasadena, CA 91109

ORDER FORM

please send _____ copies of

The Evacuation Diary of Hatsuye Egami
edited and with an introduction by Claire Gorfinkel

to: NAME _____

ADDRESS _____

CITY _____ STATE _____ ZIP _____

payment of $_____ is enclosed, or bill my

____ mastercard or ____ visa Account # _____

Name as it appears on card _____

Signature _____

COST: $15.00 per copy includes tax, postage and handling.
Ask about discounts on quantities.

ACKNOWLEDGMENTS

The Beatles said it best: "I get by with a little help from my friends" and the friends and family who help me get by are too numerous to mention here. Many people made unique contributions to the development of this manuscript, and it would not have reached its final form without their help. Special gratitude is due to Tosh Kawahara, Arline Hobson, Elizabeth Ozawa, George Egami, Louisa Egami Fujii, Judy Strasser, Lady Borton, Linda Pillsbury, George and Rosie Matsuura, Taka and Michy Nomura, Sue Kunitomi Embrey, Glenn Omatsu, James Sakoda, Peter Franck, Lucile Fessenden Dandelet, the staff of the Japanese American National Museum, my colleagues at the AFSC and my daughter Carrie Elizabeth Gorfinkel Frederick.

THE EVACUATION DIARY OF HATSUYE EGAMI

LIFE CANNOT BE INTERESTING IF ONLY IN ONE COLOR

It is one of my earliest memories: New Year's day in the early 1950s at the home of a Japanese American family somewhere in San Francisco. The huge, heavy, buffet table was laden with all kinds of strange and fascinating foods and in particular an immense whole fish, its eye still intact. Many years later I understood that these families had invited my family to celebrate with them as a way of thanking my attorney father for handling their Economic Loss Compensation Claims in the Federal Courts. Before the war they had been flower growers and nursery owners in Northern California. They were forced to abandon everything, often to unscrupulous caretakers, in the racist wartime hysteria which ultimately led to the incarceration of 120,000 men, women and children of Japanese ancestry, two thirds of whom were American citizens. My father helped them recover a small measure of financial compensation, and these New Years gatherings were my first introduction to "the internment" and America's concentration camps.

In 1992 I organized a series of events to commemorate the 50th anniversary of the American Friends Service

Committee (AFSC) in the Pacific Southwest. This entailed researching in archives for a historical publication, and rummaging through photographs for an exhibit. In a musty storage room in Pasadena, I discovered an entire file drawer on the Japanese "internment and relocation". It was filled with original photographs, scrapbooks of newspaper clippings, memoranda, correspondence, minutes from meetings, newsletters and publications documenting both the historic injustice and the unique humanitarian response. It seemed clear that these materials, which had been ignored for so long, contained a vital and compelling story. I resolved to make that story public and find a more appropriate home for the documents.

Thus, in May 1993, the AFSC in Pasadena hosted an exhibit "50 Years Later: Remembering the Japanese American Internment, from the files of the American Friends Service Committee." In putting the exhibit together I called upon members of Pasadena's Japanese American community to share their artifacts, memories and memorabilia, believing they would make the exhibit more meaningful. I also called upon members of the AFSC and the Quaker community for their recollections and artifacts.

One day the mail brought me a package from Arline Booth Hobson, an active Quaker and AFSC committee member in Tucson, Arizona. Arline's parents, G. Raymond and Gracia Booth, were among those who represented Quakers and AFSC in 1942, attending to many needs of Japanese American families as they were being rounded up. Later they were regular visitors to Tulare, Santa Anita, Manzanar and other camps, bringing messages, clothing and personal items, and contact with the outside world. Gracia Booth published several articles appealing for compassion and understanding instead of racism and injustice. She also befriended a Pasadena *Issei* woman named Hatsuye Egami who entrusted her with three chapters of the *Evacuation Diary* that she had written in Tulare. As she states in the diary, Mrs. Egami hoped her writing would one day be published and contribute to greater understanding. Her intimate personal story of departure from Pasadena, which Arline had now passed along to me, became the narrative for our exhibit.

Throughout the month of May, Japanese American visitors came every day to see our photographs, the original drawings, and other art work produced in the camps, clippings from the *Los Angeles Times* and the *Pasadena Star-News*, camp maps and newsletters, and one family's trunk with their name and number still on it. They shared their memories with me. Some discovered familiar faces in photographs that were 50 years old. Many expressed ambivalence at re-examining old hurts which they juxtaposed with the need to educate younger generations about this injustice. Over and over I heard references to Quakers: "the only ones who stood by us." or "The only presents our children got for Christmas that first year in camp came from the American Friends Service Committee." and "My first child was born in camp and the only new thing I had for her was a layette knit by some Quaker lady."

It was not until the exhibit was about to close, that I met Sue Kunitomi Embrey, a prominent activist in the Los Angeles Japanese American community who had also once volunteered with the AFSC. Like so many others who visited during the month, she spoke movingly of her experience, the 50-year-old memory of the camps still painful, and her recollection of the Quakers' contribution still powerful. Sue had an additional story. She had what she called an "unpublished novel" about a Pasadena *Issei* woman, which had been given to her by Don Rundstrom, an early member of the Manzanar Committee. She asked whether I couldn't perhaps trace the family and try to get this novel into print.

As I put her manuscript on the photocopier so I could return the precious original to her, I knew right away who the family was, for here were twelve chapters of the same diary that Arline Hobson had given me two months earlier. I felt an almost mystical calling to publish the diary which you now hold in your hands.

Why should this diary be published, more than 50 years after it was written? There are several reasons. In 1995, the same Immigration and Naturalization Service (INS) that made lists of suspects and rounded up Japanese Americans before Pearl Harbor is currently calling for stronger anti-immigrant legislation and increased militarization of our borders. Californians who voted for Proposition 187 in 1994 are projecting their fears and hostility onto persons with brown skins and Spanish-sounding surnames just as their counterparts dehumanized the Japanese of 1942. Once again, their motivations are complicated by politics and economics. The finger of blame is pointed without regard for the conditions which attract people to the United States. And while disregarding others' actual birthplace, citizenship, and real or potential contribution to society, people often forget how recently their own families were also immigrants.

There is another reason. Fifty years after the liberation of Auschwitz, Mrs. Egami's narrative carries emotional power. Here is the intimate experience of one family among thousands of people who were rounded up on the basis of race, herded onto trains, and sent off to an unknown destination from which they had no way of knowing if they would ever return. That they did, for the most part, survive the camp experience and return to productive lives does not mitigate the fundamental injustice perpetrated by our government in our name.

The Caucasian soldiers on Mrs. Egami's train may have joked and shared food with their captive passengers, but they also drew the window shades tightly shut whenever the train passed through a town. Were they protecting people from hate-filled stares and racist insults, or insuring that their passengers would not know where they were?

Camp residents were told that the tall towers with powerful searchlights and guards wielding machine guns were erected "for their own protection" but over and over again they questioned: "Why then, are the guns and the lights always pointed towards us?"

12

© Lucile Fessenden Dandelet, 1942

Japanese Americans waiting to board the train. Los Angeles, 1942

And when Mrs. Egami's daughter exclaims upon arrival at Tulare: "Mama, if we enter this gate we shall never be able to come out again until the end of the war!" how can we not recall those who did not return from the death camps of Europe? We who care about justice must continue to tell this story, and work to ensure that it does not happen again.

Mrs. Egami's diary of her evacuation is unusual in the literature of the internment. Few written records have come from the *Issei*, many of whom, like Mrs. Egami, knew little English. Most of what has been published consists of memoirs, recollections, and fictional or composite accounts from the perspective of later years. Internment accounts generally deal with the ten "permanent" camps: Gila, Granada, Heart Mountain, Jerome, Manzanar, Minidoka, Poston, Rohwer, Topaz and Tule Lake, where over 100,000 persons of Japanese ancestry waited out the remainder of the war years. In contrast, Mrs. Egami's story has immediacy: it was written as events were unfolding. The shocks of communal latrines, barracks, and dining halls, the anxieties of separation and family breakdowns, the details of social and religious life, as well as the unanticipated experiences of kindness and joy, were fresh and new when she wrote about them.

And there is one final reason for publishing Mrs. Egami's diary. Her motivation for writing was not political. She believed that injustice could be explained ("it is war, after all") and ultimately overcome by poetry and acts of kindness.

In the shock of discovering the complete lack of privacy in the women's latrines at Tulare Assembly Center, Mrs. Egami told her three daughters ". . . I think that life here is going to be largely primitive and naked. But don't you think that this is interesting too? All of you have been able to enjoy civilized life fully until now. *Life cannot be interesting if only in one color. . . .* I think that from this bare life we can weave something creative and interesting." Thus, her diary is a testimony to the little things: children and flowers, children and apricots, the 4th of July parade, her son's fifth grade class in Pasadena, the talent show, people reaching out to one another, and the human spirit that transcends adversity. In reading Mrs. Egami's diary we are reminded once again that even in the midst of unspeakable evil, acts of kindness, generosity and goodness occur.

We actually have very little concrete information about Hatsuye Egami. According to Gracia Booth, she was born in Tokyo in July, 1902, where her father was a Baptist minister. She lost her mother very early in life, graduated from the Mission School in Himeji at the age of 18 and was immediately married. An Uncle, also a Baptist minister living in America, arranged for Mrs. Egami and her family to move to the United States in 1921. Here she studied music, which she also taught until the time of the evacuation. She may have also written for the *Rafu Shimpo*, the Los Angeles Japanese daily newspaper, during that time but no one has been able to locate her work.

At the time of the evacuation, the Egami family included three daughters and one son. Only her eldest (Sachiko), and youngest (George), are mentioned by name in the Diary. Gracia Booth described the Diary writer as "a very wide-awake and energetic person. She is cheerful, ambitious, and desirous of viewing things — even a disastrous uprooting of her "growing-up" family — objectively but, at the same time, with understanding sympathy."

Gracia Booth's "biographical sketch" concludes with the words: "The following pages from her diary were translated from the Japanese by James Sakoda, a young *Nisei* psychology student from Berkeley. They were sent to me with the request that I send them to the magazine or paper where I thought they would do the most for the cause of the Japanese. When the war is won and they must return to the citizen world and re-establish themselves all over again may the poignant appeal in this record of a woman's heart-ache do good work!"

Loading up. Pasadena 1942

THE EVACUATION DIARY OF HATSUYE EGAMI

CHAPTER 1

MAY 12, 1942

Up at five. We had thrown ourselves on the hardwood floor spread with thin blankets and slept. Very simple. The fire that had burned in the fireplace the whole night through is still burning faintly. The fireplace that the whole family loved. Beside it we had talked and laughed through that last night. And must we really part from this room now?

"It's war! We can't be sentimental, we can't," I had thought, but the urge to become sentimental which I had suppressed with each event seemed to gush forth as I gazed on the fire that still continued to sparkle a bit. But that was for only a moment; I raised my eyes, gave my head a shake, and stood up, my good spirit restored.

The children woke up, too, and we all began our last preparations with much hullabaloo. Evacuation was to be carried out in three days and we were to go on the first day. Mr. Matsumoto, who lived across the street and who was to leave on the third day, came over to help us.

"Baggage is limited to the amount that can be carried in both hands", was the Army's orders. From what we had heard from people who had already evacuated, however, it seemed that, in the end, those who took a great deal had the advantage, and we certainly racked our heads about the baggage.

"This won't do. That won't do either!" we had said as we packed and repacked our bundles, and now the final results were stacked up in the living room. Just about the time preparations were done and we felt relieved, Mr. Castro, whom we were accustomed to calling in, showed his robust form, wrinkling his dark-red face into a smile. He carried off lightly the bags which my eldest daughter and I had sweated so to jam full of things and had thought so heavy!

Since yesterday, we Pasadena Japanese have ceased to be human beings — we are now simply numbers or things. We are no longer "Egamis" but the number 23324. A tag with that number is on every suitcase and bag. Even on our breasts are tied large tags with this same number — 23324! Again, a sad and tragic feeling grips my heart!

Our neighbor, Mrs. Rasparry, brings cocoa for the children and coffee for the elders. Feeling a warmth of affection, I drink the coffee. The taxi that we had called yesterday arrived at 7:15 sharp, and now we must start.

Pursuing Mr. Castro's truck, which left a moment before us, the taxi carrying our little family of six, picks up speed — we are going! Mrs. Rasparry waves her hands, as if, I thought, they would tear off, and sees us off. For five years we had lived as neighbors, forgetting racial differences entirely. As if we were relatives, we had associated with her. I don't think that we shall ever forget how much she has done for us since the evacuation problem came upon us. On May 10, Mother's Day, I sent her bright red roses. The fact that she shed tears and showed her appreciation will surely remain with us as warm memories for a long, long time.

20

CHAPTER 1 – MAY 12, 1942

At half-past seven the taxi reached California Street, where the train we were to board was lined up — car after car after car. The faces of Caucasians seemed to overflow the place. It was a deluge of sad faces. Beautiful city. Educational city. City of the Rose Parade. City that has been friendly to the Japanese to the last! This is our last morning with Pasadena! Whether we laugh or what we do — it is no use now!

We do not know at all where we are going or what is to become of us even in the next moment, but among the Japanese no one is crying. Those who are crying are rather white Americans and Negroes and "foreigners" who came to see us off. They are honest and simple. It seems that when they want to cry, they can raise their voices and cry as they wish. It is the Japanese, who are being sent off, who are consoling them!

Since December 7th, Japanese should not have shed a single tear! It has been a very hard position to maintain. The parents, mostly, are Aliens, "enemy Aliens", and the children are American citizens! Children were sent in large number to the Army, and fathers and many mothers were sent to detention camps. Those were days filled with fear. It was a long succession of cruel, sad days, but not one of us should have cried. Japanese might have been good as dead on December 7th! And you cannot expect dead people to have tears! So we too, three hundred strong, started out on our train journey without fuss.

After we determined our seats and put our baggage upon the rack and settled down, breakfast made by Christian churches and other Pasadena friends was distributed. I didn't have any appetite, but I drank some milk in order to accept the warm feelings extended.

Last night, Mr. Matsumoto said: "The Pasadena group may be split up. This may be our last night together with you." We drank coffee and talked together. Smiling cheerfully, as usual, the same Mr. Matsumoto was here with his wife, to see us off. For five years we lived across from each other, but recently, especially, we leaned on each other, and he used to come to talk with us almost every night. When will we be able to get together again?

"Let's stay fit, shall we?" Because if we're healthy, we'll be able to meet again — sometime, perhaps." So saying, we gripped each other's hands.

Here and there were faces of friends and acquaintances looking up. The sight of an American (Caucasian) girl wrapped in red slacks, rushing about to comfort us was fresh and lovely, innocent and cute. It seems that no matter how hard Japanese try, they can't express themselves in that manner. For a flash, I found myself thinking, lightly, "What an enviable trait to have!"

It's close to nine. I think, with pain, we are going to leave. The crowd begins to wave their hands, vigorously. We wave just as hard, and face after face, hills and trees, all begins to drop behind. Now the train passes streets of Pasadena where we lived and learned to love. We crossed Colorado Street. The stores where we bought so much yarn, the hotels, department stores, appear for a flash and then disappear. The faces of kind and lovely salesgirls bob up for a moment.

The children shout: "This is Michigan Street!" and hurriedly I look back, straining my eyes through tears. Michigan Street! until this morning, our beloved home street! Our house was situated near the tracks and every time a train passed by, the house shook as if there was an earthquake. Just now the train ran over those tracks — home — Michigan Street.

CHAPTER 1 — MAY 12, 1942

Pasadena. I don't think that I can forget this beautiful green town even beyond the grave. Dignified, religious, educational city of Pasadena. The graduation exercises that were held in the Rose Bowl on quiet evenings in June. What I loved most was the abundance of green trees along the streets. How well I cherished the maple trees near our home! It was a street fully lined with maple trees. I liked it especially in May, after the trees had stood pointing heavenward all winter, as if sketched in ink. Then they suddenly burst into fresh verdure all at once. I walked this street when my mind became tired. The soft verdure of the street enveloped me like the gentle love of a mother.

When I heard that in the City Council there was a resolution against the Japanese, I thought "This in Pasadena!" and felt very sad. But the next day an opposite resolution was passed because it was Pasadena. Dr. Harbeson, president of Pasadena Junior College, Dr. and Mrs. Millikan of Caltech and others deserved respect and possessed admirable characters. They worked for our cause bravely. For their wonderful attitude and clear conviction I bow my head The Japanese will certainly remember them forever.

It is war! Why should I complain now? Verdant Pasadena — I shall surely love Pasadena forever.

The train speeds along. In a moment the city streets are passed, and in both windows, gradually, desert-like scenery unfolds. It might have been only my imagination, but the temperature surely rises. The strain which has been accumulating since December 7th seems to weigh upon body and soul, all at once. Among the adults there are some who are slumped in their seats like weakened fishes, imbibing sleep. There cheerful ones are the youngsters. They are raising a rumpus as if they were on a picnic.

The train weaves in and out between hills after hills and runs along. On the mountains the greenness becomes less and, gradually, the desert seems to increase its expansiveness. I notice people on the wayside taking off their hats and waving politely. Becoming tearful, I wave my hand with all my might. But this becomes gradually less. About noon, lunch boxes are passed out by the soldiers: milk, sandwiches, oranges, cake. It's quite a feast.

The train runs on. It continues to advance into the famous and expansive Mohave Desert. Presently, we pass places where water is trickling in the creek. Pretty mountain birds are gathered cheerfully. In the green meadows cows are grazing and, above, white clouds are floating gently. In contrast to the giant cacti that could be mistaken for large trees, that I gazed on with surprise, I find wild flowers whose names I don't know, smiling at me. While nation fights nation, and people kill each other and suffer, how peaceful nature is. Was nature always so peaceful and so immense and so beautiful as this? I gazed as if for the first time.

I hear a burst of joyous laughter, and turn around. Four or five pretty girls are talking with some soldier-boys and they are laughing together wholesomely. These seem to be harmless and cute soldiers. I would not like to see these innocent soldiers sent to war to be killed or maimed.

CHAPTER 1 — MAY 12, 1942

The train carrying its load of disturbed thoughts finally approaches its destination. The sun of the desert suddenly disappears, and the surroundings are enveloped in a grayish dusk. The journey required eleven hours, and it is about eight PM. Tulare at last. People are looking out of the windows and I do so, too. Beyond the road by the tracks there is a place that looks like a race-track. The grandstand is filled with Japanese, clustered together, silently, like ants. Can it be that those who arrived in the Assembly Center before us are out to welcome us newcomers?

The train comes to a standstill. Those in the front car begin to get off in an orderly way. Our historic entrance into an internment camp has begun. As I am in the last car, I observe the line quietly. Mothers with children in their arms, sturdy youths, tottering old men leaning on sticks, cheerful children, beautiful lasses — I was too far off to see the facial expression of each person, but the flow of the moving human line, how silent and gloomy!

The wave of the line flows gently along. And pretty soon our family, too, becomes one more wave in the silent stream and we find ourselves slowly moving forward. I am carrying two suitcases and a blanket. The camp lies beyond the road, and, as soldiers guard us, we reach the gate.

Tulare Assembly Center!

My eldest daughter says, "Mama, if we enter this gate we shall never be able to come out again until the end of the war!" It seems so obvious, but no one laughs. Someone answered: "Really, let's remember this feeling. This is probably an event we shall never experience again during our lifetime." In the next moment we finally pass the gate and become residents of the Center.

The gloomy feeling that gripped me on entering the Center is soon blown away. Ovations and shouts that pieced the sky await us. On both sides of the road a human fence, so tight that it seems that an ant would not have been able to get through, was erected by Japanese already in. As if we were generals back from war or something, we walk between the road lined with people.

There seems to be no one that I know. But it is a whirlpool of faces dear to me, as if I knew them intimately. Suddenly, I see Mr. U. who turns his thoughtful face toward me, and is waving at me. Something warm rises up in my breast, and I swallow.

After I walk a little way, there is someone who shouts, "Egami-san!" I look around. Why, it is Mr. Miura. He is fat as he always was, and as usual he lights up his round face with a smile. Miura-san: I thought all along that he had gone to Santa Anita, but he's been here. He appreciated my poor artistic ability, understood my nature well, loved me as a sister regardless of my strong and weak points. Miura-san is here. I become cheerful and brighten up, and with light steps I walk on.

It is already past ten when baggage inspection and other things are over, and we finally step into our new home. Its name is L-8-3. It is a rustic barrack of rough boards put together with five windows and a concrete floor. There are Army cots and khaki blankets in the room. Eight people occupy our room.

Young men who preceded us here are busily helping with the baggage and other things as if in a contest. As soon as we arrive, the people next door console us: "You must be tired. I'm glad you've come." Everyone is friendly and kind. We unpack our baggage, take out our bedding, and together, we noisily make our beds.

26

CHAPTER 1 – MAY 12, 1942

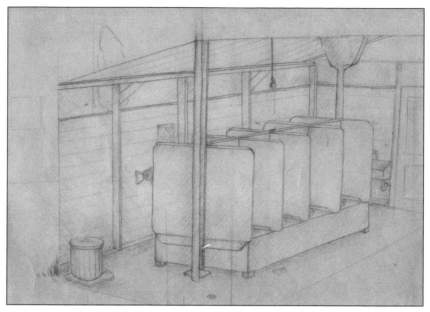

Women's latrines, Tulare Assembly Center
by Shigeko Elizabeth Ozawa, August 1, 1942

Guided by a neighbor, all of us go to the latrine, which is about a block away. As soon as we enter, my daughters shriek. I could not help become wobbly and stare before me. I indeed felt sorry for my daughters. In the latrine the cloak of modesty must be shed and we must return to the state of nakedness in which we were born. Polished civilized taste and fine sensitivity seem to have become worthless here.

But I turned to my daughters and told them sincerely, "When people return to a state of nakedness, their true worth becomes evident. I think that life here is going to be largely primitive and naked. But don't you think that this is interesting, too? All of you have been able to enjoy civilized life fully until now. Life cannot be interesting if only in one color. It is like a design created by variegated colored strands woven together. It may be that in a naked life there is poetry and truth. I think that from this bare life we can weave something creative and interesting. The person that can do that is one who is really intelligent and wise. Let's carve out a good life together."

Having said this, gradually I became more cheerful. We returned to our room and threw our tired bodies and souls on our beds.

CHAPTER II

It is morning in the camp. Accompanied by noisy feet and voices of people, I open my eyes. I go to the washroom. Those that I know and I do not know, all smile and say "good morning" when I meet them.

At the mess-hall, which holds 160 persons, 500 are waiting their turn in line. The wave of the line flows on for about a block, and I take my place with the others. Mothers with children in their arms, tottering old men, all quietly stand in line. The refreshing morning breeze brushes the skin pleasantly. I enter the mess-hall. In cafeteria fashion, by the entrance, we pick up our own knives, forks, and spoons and plates and move ahead. Grapefruits, mush, boiled eggs, toast, butter. On the rectangular table are placed large pitchers of coffee and milk, also salt, pepper, cream, *shoyu* and the like.

At noon we usually have soup, rice, salad and perhaps beans. For dinner there is usually meat of some sort or fish and such dessert as cake, pie or pudding. To the Japanese who were used to eating well, this might not be a feast; on the other

Serving table of mess hall, Tulare Assembly Center
by Shigeko Elizabeth Ozawa

hand, it is certainly not so bad as to deserve complaints. To children under 13, milk is given, and special diets are being contemplated for pregnant women and those who are ill.

This is a cooperative community of several thousand people. The taste and whim of individuals cannot always be given due consideration. The administration at least, is doing its best for us. That effort we should always take in a good way.

In a camp it can be said that food above all things, is the center and the pleasure of life. It's natural to want to eat something good. I cannot help thinking about the old men standing with plates in their hands. Residents in America for forty or fifty years, they pursued gigantic dreams and crossed an expansive ocean to America to live. The soil they tilled was a mother to them, and their life was regulated by the sun. They were

people who had worked with all they had, until on their fore-
heads, wave-like furrows were harrowed. Every time I see these
oldsters with resigned, peaceful expressions, meekly eating what
is offered them, I feel my eyes become warm. However, when I
see the young people always complaining at every meal, my
spirits are low. And as for these people who maliciously twist
things, and, for instance, create bad rumors, I cannot help feeling even hateful toward them. I want to keep my outlook in
sharp focus. No matter what we are up against, I don't want to
see things through distorted lenses. I want to maintain a fair
and just attitude. Every time I eat, I am moved to feel in that
way. In times like these, especially, this is my greatest desire.

A messenger came from Mr. Miura. I go to his office. As I
walk between rows of similar barracks and come out
where the grandstand is, I find the administration headquarters.
This seems to be divided into many departments. In the center, the grandstand sits solidly, and Mr. Aanonsen is the manager. Surrounding it there are such departments as the Works
Maintenance Division, Service Division, Finance and Records
Division, Lodging and Mess Division, and these in turn are sub-
divided in smaller branches. Mr. Miura's Social Welfare
Division is a branch of the Service Division, and that is where I
was taken.

The Social Welfare Division looks after the welfare of the
camp, such as marriage, birth, death, family problems, social
case work, sickness, transfer, Red-Cross work, knitting, first-aid,
women's problems, religious problems, juvenile problems, moral
problems, financial advice. Mr. Miura is in charge, and efficient *Niseis* are working under him.

I don't know a thing about other offices, but as I go to
Mr. Miura's office almost every day, I have gradually become

familiar with his personnel. It is a happy coincidence that Mr.
Tamura's wife is a daughter of Mr. Sasaki, a close literary friend
of mine. Mr. Tamura is a calm splendid young man. You would
not think that Mrs. Nishimura was a mother of three, from her
youthfulness and efficient and bright mind. I like her. Helen
Kimura, Kimi Sakanishi, Kimi Ishii, Bob Takahashi and others
are all loving people and I began to enjoy more and more going
to Mr. Miura's office.

Mr. Miura seems to be enjoying his life very much. It's
because his socially-ideal life is actually being practiced. He is
always busily, but cheerfully going this way and that.

Five thousand people: this is quite a town. Crime,
tragedy, comedy—it certainly should have all of the elements
for all sorts of social problems. Every day all sorts of problems
arise; and since the town is a special one, the problems too,
take on peculiar forms and shades of color. They should certainly present interesting social phenomena. I shall pick up
some of the stories from among those that have trickled out of
Mr. Miura's office.

Around the camp fences have been erected, and about the
fence watch-towers have been set up, with soldiers standing guard 24 hours a day. But the soldiers seem to be admirable
and innocent. Even though a fence is there, no one tries to get
out. Since it's so peaceful and uneventful, I almost feel like
asking whether the soldiers are bored. Far away from home,
separated from people they love, these young men must certainly feel lonely. These youths are pure. In their spare moments
when they look at us, especially pretty *Nisei* girls — wouldn't
they think of us, not as enemy aliens, but rather as pitiful and
touching captives? So soldiers must have looked at the girls
with loving eyes, and perhaps done something kind for them,
which the lasses innocently accepted.

CHAPTER 11

In this way, the seed of love began to germinate between a soldier and a certain girl. At dawn (around four or five o'clock), the girl went to the fence where the soldier was to meet her. Wartime rules, however are uncompromising. They are extremely strict. We are not allowed to speak to anyone outside the fence — especially soldiers.

Mr. Miura was troubled with this problem, and so were the Center policemen. But it was solved rather simply. In order to plant flowers, the patch of ground next to the fence was spaded up. Dark, wet dirt — the fence could not be approached without becoming dirty. Without hurting anyone's feelings, without bothering anyone, the solution to the problem was intelligent and full of human understanding. Every time I see the spaded up dark earth by the fence, I cannot help smiling.

THE EVACUATION DIARY OF HATSUYE EGAMI

CHAPTER III

SUNDAY MORNING

We are to have Sunday morning service in Camp. I change my clothes, take my bible and hymnal and start for the grandstand. The sky above is a vivid blue. It is indeed a radiant morning. The young girls have abandoned slacks and their week-day camp attire and this morning I see them in their Sunday best. The young men too are in their suits, but their fineries of normal days are not to be seen. Little tots in red or yellow sweaters flit about full of life and gaiety like colorful butterflies.

I seat myself on the grandstand. This little town that holds 5,000 people can be seen from here in a single glance. Outside our enclosure are trees. Their boughs are so inter-locked that it appears as though this camp were surrounded by a cool woodland. Over the tree tops, birds flash by. From this dreamy reverie, I am awakened.

The service has begun. "Holy, holy, holy . . ." comes the familiar strain. Everyone is singing. They are singing with all their might. Their faces are very earnest. The very heights and depth of spiritual feeling radiates their countenance. I too, strain my voice to its limit and sing. Others in Santa Anita, and Manzanar too, must be singing just as we are. Prayers of deep reverence are being uttered in their midst too, I know. Songs, voices, resound to the limits of heaven! As we sang, my eyelids began to burn.

Reverend Hunter, a minister from Hollywood and one who is also a famous writer, has come today to speak to us. "At every meal, instead of our usual grace, we bow our heads to visualize the long line at meal time and the patient faces of those that stand in line at every center." These were the worlds he uttered. That one thought . . . it was not just the kind words, but his sincere attitude and humility vibrated even to us who understood so little of his speech.

> "How can we help it, this is war.
> I mustn't shed tears.
> I mustn't weaken.
> I mustn't be fussy.
> I mustn't expect sympathy.
> I must brace myself!
> I must smile!"

This is the position we Japanese must take to heart. Brace myself as I will, his words of sympathy, warm understanding and a revelation of the beauty of his soul continue to vibrate upon my ear. Tears well up from the deep recesses of my soul.

At the same instant, I thought "There must be a number of American prisoners confined in Japan — Americans in combat on the battlefields of Asia. There must be some lying mortally wounded out on the fields or confined in hospitals. Just as the people must suffer from this war, Christians the world-over, I know, are joined in song and prayer at this very hour.

CHAPTER III — SUNDAY MORNING

Notices are posted on every mess-hall door. "May 18, 8:00 PM, Mrs. Michiko Toguri's Funeral at L-4." This is the first funeral to be held in Camp. She is a total stranger to me. I have never heard her name, but why I must I remain a stranger to her? For I have boarded the same ship of destiny with her, to live, to die. Such common threads of fate that hold us together must not keep us apart.

There is a piano in L-4. It is an Assembly Hall. People holding the same common thought for this one who went on before us, gather within the walls of this barrack. The interior of this hall is the very extreme of plainness. Each rough board is separated with an obvious space. The floor, the ceiling, the seats and table, all are of this unplaned lumber with no evidence of refinement.

Before the coffin, there is a pitifully small amount of flowers. The evidences of finesse and refinement that we were accustomed to before, are not to be found. I played the piano. It too, was dust-covered, out of tune and difficult to play. Even so, I played for all my worth. Fingers, break if they must! Playing at funerals is so familiar, I have lost count. I have played before coffins that were buried with expensive floral wreaths, where the piano was an expensive instrument in excellent condition, but have I ever played with such fervor as today?

Words of condolence took wing and struck our heart strings as one after another gave words of sympathy or offered their prayers. All the ritual, ceremony and complicated forms connected with such occasions cannot be eliminated. All visible shape and appearance of each preceding occasion seems like empty shells. So long as these occasions were predominated by such ritualism, the sincerity of feeling that should have been there was missing.

Births, deaths, marriages: such occasions have necessitated spending an enormous sum of money. The Japanese could not remedy this social burden and cancer for it prevails in our former Japanese society. So this is an unexpected revolution. It is indeed, wonderful progress! Just a simple funeral attended with sincerity of thought. Here and there I can hear the quiet sobbing of people. From the beginning to the very close, I too have cried. It was truly an unforgettable funeral.

I go out of doors. This is early summer. The night sky is beautiful. The stars are so clear, and brilliant they seem to pierce the sky. The atmosphere too is clear. I watch the figures of many others who walk 'neath this nocturnal scene. As I mechanically plod along, my mind continues to revert to the funeral. That throng was total strangers. Unfinished simple barrack, such a pitiful showing of flowers, but sincerity pervaded and tears flowed that night. Weren't they a far more priceless offering to the spirit of the one who left our midst?

After breakfast, I carry my large bundle of soiled clothing to the community laundry. Just as showers are placed in the center of one unit, so there is one laundry. Double basins of concrete line both walls and every place is occupied. I see people performing a necessary duty cheerfully. Because no place is to be had, I stand and wait awhile.

On the wall to the left of me hangs a notice:

NOTICE

This laundry is not a private one. Certain inconveniences must be borne. First, there is a lack of hot water, so please rinse with cold water. After you are through, please clean each basin.

If there are scraps of paper or litter on the floor, please place them in the waste box. Help us maintain cleanliness.

Sanitary Committee

CHAPTER III — SUNDAY MORNING

Having read this notice, I looked about me and to my surprise could not see a single strip of paper. It was indeed a clean laundry room. In the latrines and in the mess-halls, I have seen similar notices. In such a crowded community, the greatest care and precaution must be enforced. Until now, I have not noticed how well these rules of sanitation have been adhered to.

"From now on, this is to be our home. Let us help to make it as comfortable as possible." That seems to be the common thought of every one.

From time to time the occupant of each basin changes. This duty of washing, once considered a woman's duty, has certainly changed. In many instances, husbands are lending a hand, and in some cases, a son is seen beside his mother helping.

One must walk a full block to the laundry, then carry the wet wash back a block to hang out on the lines. Really, it is quite an ordeal. It used to be, if we turned a switch, the washer went around and around, then just a step or two to hang out the wash — such convenience and ease has changed dramatically.

The men are bored, so it must be a good exercise for them to put in a helping hand. "Other husbands help with the family laundry. Why can't you help me too?" Not caring to be outdone by other wives, I called my husband. I wash. The master rinses and takes the wash to put on the line.

The water here is surprisingly soft. "Regardless of temperature, the water here suds easily, so the laundry comes out very white" remarked of one of my neighbors. A friend of mine leaned over toward my basin and whispered, "The snow that caps the Sierra Nevada range throughout the year melts and comes here, that is why the water is so soft."

Dusty roads. Dusty room. Everything is dust-covered: clothing, bedding, our body. Everything soils so easily, it seems washing must be done daily. Everyone without exception is seen in such neatly ironed clothes. Children, infants, all have such crisp-clean clothing. Occasionally patches are seen and their garments may be faded, but even then, they are immaculately clean.

In the open row between barracks, ropes or wires are strung, and on them hangs the fresh washing. They are fluttering in the breeze. I am suddenly filled with cheer as I gaze upon the varicolored garments that string across the line as the flag of nations at some festive occasion.

There is no line discriminating rich or poor.
There is no class.
There is no political nor economic position.
There is no intellectual clique.
The difference or the importance of sex has been erased.
The privileged or the humble mass are alike.
Everything has been leveled off.

There is a former nurseryman who enjoyed a $2,000 monthly income. Now he is responsible for dealing out the milk to children under 12 years of age at each meal time. These smiling youngsters like this man who gives them their milk. He too, loves to serve these innocent ones. His duty brings happiness to them, therefore he enjoys his work.

Another man was the proprietor of a large hotel. Today he is a carpenter. Garbed as a carpenter, shouldering his box of tools, I see him as he trudges by each day. Then there is a former principal of a language school, a man of exceptional character, respected for his resourcefulness. He was once interned, but now he has returned to this Center and is a janitor in the infirmary.

40

CHAPTER III — SUNDAY MORNING

Once the proprietor of a prosperous laundry, another man now spends his day as a gardener. Deeply tanned, he works beneath the burning heat of the day. Then there is the former operator of a large chop suey parlor. He is now cook in one of the kitchens where it is very hot because coal is used for heat. When I see him around 7:00 each morning, his shirt is drenched with perspiration. Even so, he works without grudging.

What I have so far cited, pertains to the elders — our first generation, but the same applies to the young people too. There are approximately 100 young people in the administration office, working intently over their desks and typewriters each day. Whether it regards mail, the fire department, street sanitation, maintenance, or the kitchens, countless boys and girls are at work. In the kitchen, amid confusion that could be compared to a battle, in that bustle and hurry, deftly they perform their tasks.

In every imaginable field, their work of serving the community is revealed. This is but a rough sketch of this, our world. In this unique community, no one is compelled to work, but in spite of this complete disregard for privilege or class, workers are the first to eat. Selfishness, egotism, or cunning, all such characteristics are shoved aside as unfit. The spirit of charity and cooperation is necessary.

Those who possess beauty of soul, or who are blessed with the gift of creativeness, are able to turn these unfavorable circumstances into a rich experience. People such as these, are wealthy, are indeed blessed, are happy, for to them defeat is something unknown. I disagree with much of the Communistic doctrine, but life in this community seems to reveal the best that it possesses. Life in such a state holds the possibilities of establishing utopia. If conditions continue to progress and improve in the course of years, we may create a beautiful example to present to our outer world.

THE EVACUATION DIARY OF HATSUYE EGAMI

CHAPTER IV

MAY 31, 1942

I joined in the Memorial Day ceremony that was held in front of the grandstand, amidst a throng like a human tidal wave. There was hardly room to insert a splinter.

The blazing hot sun as it took its course toward the West quietly sank beyond the horizon. In the light of the afterglow, people's faces revealed a mixture of memories of the past and feelings aroused by the ceremony they were witnessing. Directly before the grandstand was a truck on which there was a piano. In front of the truck stood officers, Boy Scouts, veterans of the last war (about ten Japanese) and participants in today's program.

The center section of the grandstand was occupied by parents and family of those who are now in the armed forces of this country. A lovely floral wreath which was presented by the Police Department stood in the center of the stage. At 7:30 sharp, three boy Scouts presented the colors. The audience stood at attention and recited the Pledge of Allegiance.

A prayer was offered by Reverend Susu-Mago, who represented the *Nisei*. A vocal solo of the Star Spangled Banner was rendered by Mrs. May Takasugi. It was lovely. Her voice was beautiful and her grace and poise gave a wonderful impression to the listening audience.

Last March, at the Pasadena Junior College annual Music Spring Festival, Mrs. Takasugi and the PJC Orchestra created such an impressive close. All its beauty and impressiveness was brought back to me. In every line and walk of life, gifted young people were just beginning to open their buds. This young artist was one of them. In fact, she was one of the outstanding in their midst.

Under these circumstances, we are plainly branded as enemy aliens and enemy nationals. That is why we are in these enclosures, but our devotion and loyalty to this country is unchanged.

Mrs. Takasugi's clear voice, as she sang the anthem, pierced our hearts. Next, Mrs. Susu-Mago read a poem written by George Elliot. Mrs. Susu-Mago is a Caucasian-American. Her father is a professor at the University of Southern California. She is the wife of a Japanese and is confined here just as one of us. There seem to be several similar cases here of mixed marriages. Love seems to surmount all barriers and outshine all the troubles of this world. Wars, discrimination among races; these individuals were able to overcome all these to live in a universal love.

The veterans of the last war were introduced. Each, as he was called, arose and answered with a salute. Among them, Mr. Mitsumori of Pasadena, one of my closest friends, is a perfect example as a Christian. While serving in the forces, he was loved and respected by his superiors as well as his buddies. Even after his return, his character and his faith continued unchanged. For many years he was a pillar of the Japanese Union Church of Pasadena and he served as an elder in the session.

During the war, Mr. Mitsumori was gassed. His lung was affected, but today he is completely recovered. Besides his many Church duties, he is a local advisor. His service was so much in demand that he had hardly time to sleep. When evacuation orders descended, Mr. Mitsumori was considered exempt with permission to remain behind in Pasadena. He replied that he must not be made an exception and today he is living in this Camp. As he stood at attention, these thoughts passed through my mind. With deep sincerity, I bowed my head.

Next, parents of boys who are now in the Army were introduced. In the evening breeze, the American flag curled and lashed at its string. Veterans of foreign wars, parents of the boys in uniform. . . when these aged parents stood at their seats, I could not control the hot tears that coursed down my cheek. In all the twenty years of my life here in the United States, this Memorial Day service was the most solemn and the most unforgettable.

I have just had my lunch. Upon returning to my room, I find a parcel and four or five letters. Just as we look forward to meal time, so we anticipate arrival of each mail. Thus, even the poorest correspondent turns to letter writing in his idle hours. Frugal though we aim to be, we discover that our stamp bill amounts to a surprising sum.

Our package is from Henry in Manzanar to my eldest daughter. Our curiosity is aroused. Feverishly we unwrap the bundle. As we uncover the box, a tiny pair of wooden *geta* come dancing from within. This was sent in time for Sachi's birthday which is June 4. Two or three days ago, Sachi received a letter from her friend in Manzanar. "Henry came to borrow our carpenter tools. We thought perhaps he was planning on making something for your birthday though we didn't ask him. I think you can look forward to receiving something very soon".

Surely it was so. In our camp life, this peculiar wooden-clog has become a necessity. It all takes me back to childhood days in Japan when with flowered kimono, I ran about wearing *geta*. For those who return to their homeland after many years, the first sound to remind them of being on Japanese soil is the *kara-koro* sound of many *getas* on the streets. They had forgotten that sound. It shows to what degree these Japanese had been Americanized. What we considered a mere novelty on this soil has now become so indispensable in our present daily life.

Sachi's *geta* is tiny and very dainty. On the smooth-surfaced top, burned in with the electric needle was the neat lettering, 'SACHIKO'. The straps were made of his discarded necktie of black and red stripes.

Just beyond the white-capped high Sierra range, we know that Henry is there. He went among the first volunteers that formed the vanguard to Manzanar. What were Henry's thoughts as he painstakingly fashioned this pair of clogs? Of course, Henry is Sachiko's fiance.

Over a period of years of our acquaintance, neither Sachi nor I suspected his feeling for her. That is the sort of reserved individual he is. He is a man of few words. He is well-mannered. His interests are steeped in music, literature and the finer arts. On the other hand he is scientifically minded and skillful as a radio technician. His present ambition is to study medicine. He is tall with clear-cut features. I had been fond of

Henry, for he is a fine gentleman. He was Sachi's friend and he frequented our home.

The day before his departure for Manzanar, he had come and had supper with us. Even then, he bade us farewell with no special words nor special attention for Sachiko. Two weeks after his arrival there, an especially thick letter came from him. *Over a long period of time, I have secretly admired and loved your Sachiko. Whether she loves me, I do not know, but I do know that she does not dislike me. Undeserving though I am, if my request for Sachiko's hand receives the consent of her parents, it would fill me with the greatest joy. I would then consider myself the luckiest man on earth. I would put forth every effort to study and to succeed in my undertakings for Sachiko's happiness.*

From between each word seeped through his strength and sincerity. Even the feelings that could not be shaped in words tugged at my heart as I read. With an indescribable warmth rising in my breast, I called Sachiko. "A letter has come from Henry." I showed her the missive.

"Will you think this through quietly and give Mother your most honest reply? In our life, marriage is the greatest decision. It does not concern someone else, but it concerns you. The most important elements to be considered in marriage are, first: love, next: respect for one another. Search your soul to see whether through the years you will continue to love and respect Henry and tell Mother without hesitation." Thus, I made an effort to diagnose Sachiko's feelings.

I have reared my children and trained them to this day to tell me every problem. Rather than be considered a Mother to my children, I have striven to be thought of as their best friend so that I might mingle in their world. That is why I have gone to movies and concerts with them. On our way home from a movie, we would analyze the personality of a character or the psychological reaction of the hero of the story.

As my daughters chose their boy friends, they would bring them home where I enjoyed their company. Therefore, I am confident that my girls know the type that I would prefer because of the understanding that exists between us. I myself trust the taste of my children in making their selections; therefore, I know that I can learn to like their friends. If their friendship progressed to a state of betrothal, I am positive that the fiance is a gentleman.

This understanding between my children and me is not only trust. I rather think I can compare it to faith. So, if my daughter gives her consent, she has my heart-felt approval. Sachiko was in deep thought, but she finally replied, "Up until now, I hadn't suspected, but if he loves me as he says, and since it is Henry who is asking me, I would gladly answer yes."

In the evening, I revealed the story to my husband. The following morning, I wrote Henry. That is how the two became affianced. Daily letters are exchanged between them. I watch this intercourse with parental pride and love. The problem that interferes is this war.

Where Pasadena would be evacuated, no one knew at the time. How many years we would be confined we knew not. If my daughter cannot go to Manzanar to join Henry, they would be separated for the duration. As we lived in suspense, almost daily, I have tried to strengthen my daughter's morale by reminding her that though we may be sent elsewhere, and though she must wait for the end of war, the decision she had made and the vows she had exchanged with Henry must never change. "If your engagement period lengthens, won't you take it as an opportunity to nourish and to refine this love that exists between you two?"

There seems to be no other way for me as a Mother, to comfort or to console her restless soul. Events had turned out that we could not go to Manzanar. Even though the High Sierras separate these two camps, these two young hearts pray for the early arrival of peace.

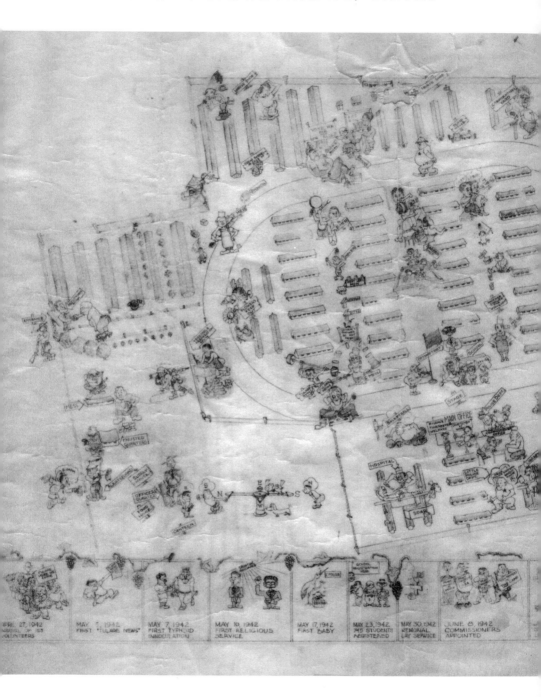

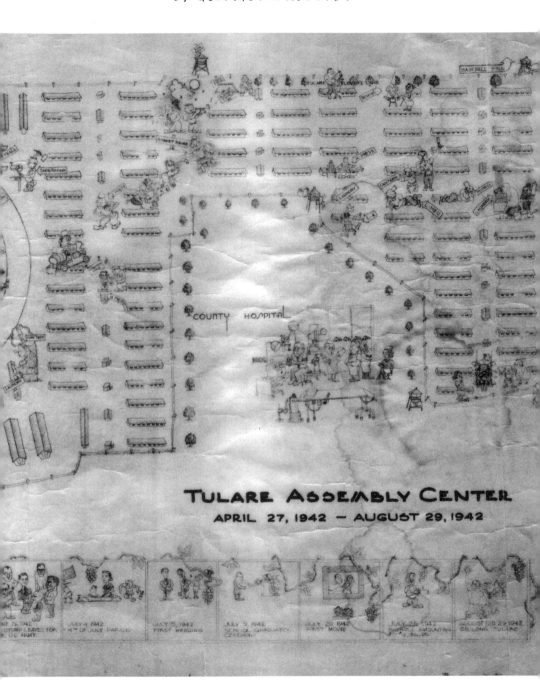

THE EVACUATION DIARY OF HATSUYE EGAMI

CHAPTER V

To my youngest son who is eleven years of age, came a letter from one of his "gang" in Pasadena. My son was, incidentally, the only Japanese student at Jefferson Grammar School where he was loved by everyone. He was a member of a group that included children from the upper social strata of Pasadena. He was especially blessed for having attended this school. The parents of his schoolmates were sure to invite George over on week-ends to baseball games or to theaters.

When war was declared on December 7, the fear that gripped my heart was for the future of my children. These children are so innocent of the woes of this world — I did not care to see them lose faith in their fellow men. The day after Pearl Harbor, when my child returned from school, I searched his face for symptoms of suffering perhaps as a physician probes for the signs of trouble in his patient.

Search as I would, not a mite of change could I discern. The 9th and the 10th came, but each day, still no signs of trouble. In fact these Caucasian boys who frequented our house even before the fateful 7th, continued to come, and George

continued to go to their homes. When evacuation orders
loomed ominously over our horizon, the friendly attentions
only seemed to intensify, and their deeds of kindness increased.

Just at that time, the China Relief Campaign was in full
swing. George's school also joined in with their contributions.
George was the school-wide Secretary for this Campaign. At
its close, he and the other officers took the total contributions
to the bank as they had been instructed. The sum of $37.00 or
so consisted of pennies, nickels and dimes. Because the poor
teller spent a tedious half hour computing this amount, it
became the source of humorous comment throughout the bank.

This mountain of coins was converted into a check. The
class officers, including George and their teacher Miss Pitts,
went to the Pasadena *Star News* office to present their bit.
Upon their arrival, they were greeted by an elegantly gowned
Chinese maiden. As George was presenting the check, a photo
was taken of the scene. The following day, it appeared in the
Star News. This, naturally brought a feeling of gratitude and
joy to me, knowing the difficulty of our circumstance. Our
phone was busy with remarks from our many Caucasian friends.

Evacuation orders were gradually creeping up on
Pasadena, and our stay in our lovely city was becoming short.
One day, George returned home from school bearing a box tied
profusely with pink ribbons. "Mother, open it please," he said.
I opened it. As I peeled off the layers of wrapping, a Van de
Kamp's box of chocolate was revealed along with a lovely card.
On top in golden letters were the words, "Friendly Greetings".

Within was the following printed verse:

"Friendship and you. There's joy behind
  That simple little phrase;
Friendship and you — Therein I find
  The gold of happy days!"

On the opposite page were these words from his teacher:

"We are going to miss you, George. Write to us.
  Love and best wishes,
  Ruth H. Pitts
  Jefferson School, March 1942

The back page was literally covered horizontally, vertically and otherwise with the signatures of his kind classmates. The warm and sincere feelings expressed, caused me to crumble into a fit of tears. The gift, considering its market value, was not much, but the thoughts that prompted the giving were priceless to me.

The next day, to show my appreciation, I sent a very humble gift. This gift was plaster of paris cast, painted a pale green, and shaded with gold. An immortal epitaph of Beethoven's words ran thus:

  "Truth exists for the wise
  And Beauty for the suggestible heart."
                              Von Beethoven

This plaque was my treasured possession. In sieges of sickness when I was confined in the hospital, I took it with me and had it on the wall where I could gaze upon those words.

The fear that almost paralyzed my senses on December 7, caused me much shame as the ensuing weeks rolled by. Friendship only proved sound and unchanged despite the sudden turn of world events. Still I brooded over erasing the innocent American spirit of boyhood that regulated George's life. At his age, he was still unconscious of racial barriers.

The staunchness of George's friends proved to me the extraordinary ability of his teachers and the refined background from which his classmates came. The beauty, culture and refinement that existed among the parents was truly reflected in these innocent children. The catastrophes that beset us often reveal hidden treasures. So, through my son and his school experiences, I have come to see an angle of American tolerance and understanding. I have come to respect this usually hidden trait that daily pulsates in America.

The fact that George must be torn from his innocent school associates and be thrown among these tired-faced evacuees — to enter these enclosures wherein are only Japanese faces — what an inexplicable disaster in his young life! As a mother I cannot help but feel sympathy for his wounded heart. However, it is my prayer that as he survives this storm and as he matures, he will be educated to hate war and its by-products. In fact I hope sincerely that as he enters manhood he will be an avowed peace advocate.

CHAPTER VI

JUNE 5, 1942

An event which the whole community anticipated with interest — the first Talent Show — has finally come. Immediately after supper, I hurried to the grandstand with my neighbors. It was to begin at 7:30, so thinking we had ample time, we leisurely approached the vicinity of the stand. To our amazement we saw an endless line like an Obi that had been carelessly flung out across the open terrain.

Humans standing in line. If one were asked to give a brief, limited description of life in this Center, that is all I could say. Meal time, post office, shower, laundry, and all other similar activities that constitute our day, one must politely await his turn. To ignore such rules and step in ahead of others is not tolerated. On burning hot afternoons there have been times when we have had to wait patiently outside the crowded canteen to buy our soothing cold drinks.

Autos, streetcars or buses are not to be found. Wherever we go, we must walk the entire distance. Even a single errand consumes a surprising amount of time. Our life of confinement might be deplorably boring, but it is surprising how quickly the close of the day overtakes us. Even now in serpentine fashion, people stand waiting to be admitted to the grandstand. These people stand uncomplaining beneath the "white hot heat" of the afternoon sun. The air is extremely dry and as I gaze about me, the green leaves of the trees appear partially wilted.

The time finally came to admit the anxious throng. As I viewed the grandstand from below, the tiny figures of people swarming onto the seats was like an avalanche suddenly released. Rather than descending, this human avalanche swarmed upward. The already hoarse-voiced, dust-covered, perspiring ushers' pleas went unheeded. The joyous throng behaved like a mad river that had found a weak spot in the dam and revelled as it broke through the opening to freedom. I too was sucked into this human whirlpool and was surprised to find myself seated like the rest in the grandstand.

Today has been exceptionally hot. "It was 114 degrees today," said my friend who sat beside me. Just as ants swarm upon sugar, and as a thirst-parched throat yearns for water, so the people have sought every cool or shady spot all afternoon. From my vantage point, I can see human specks still coming from the shelters of their barracks, or from the protecting shade of trees along the road. A surprising number of people are abandoning the concealing folds of these shady nooks. Just as these human specks have sought the cool shade today, so they seem to come here seeking another satisfaction through amusement.

A former veteran Hollywood character by the name of Tetsu Komai is directing this Talent Show. To the waiting multitude time lags, so the younger element begins a storm of hand-clapping interspersed with shrill whistling. The hot sun's strength seems to be spent and as it tips decidedly to the west the reddened rays bathe the make-shift stage.

The show finally started, as a brisk evening breeze also began to blow. Piano numbers, vocal selections, Japanese folk dance, Hawaiian music, each followed and picked up momentum. Likewise the breeze increased its strength and turned into a strong wind. The striped curtain that veiled the stage between each number flapped noisily. Each strong blast of wind disrupted the poorly erected equipment, and stole the plaintive musical notes from the straining ears of the audience.

The master of ceremonies interrupted the program to request that all firemen meet in front of the fire station because the wind had threatened the safety of the flimsy buildings. Despite such interference, the talent show continued.

Once unconsciously, I gazed heavenward to see the stars beaming unruffled from their lofty heights. The wind may blow, and dust clouds may rise, still those heavenly bodies continued to cast earthward their dancing light.

As each number closed, it was received with the same indiscriminate applause, thundering and challenging the growing gusts of wind. It did not impress me as being necessarily an indication of appreciation. Rather those outbursts seemed to me a release of pent-up emotions of joy, but also of sorrow. This is how much these people have been hungering for some form of pleasure.

I recall the figure of a certain man. Every morning this same man remained at a particular spot for some time. I know now what he was studying so intently. It has turned out to be a solitary ant-hole. For a week since I noticed him, he has kept his vigil over this tiny hole. When I discovered the object of his daily observation, I immediately thought of a book *Life of Ants* which I once read. The author is a writer of fiction, and also a naturalist. To the readers he revealed in great detail the mysteries of this common insect. Because I have not made the effort to speak to this observer of ants, I do not know whether he is scientifically-minded or whether he has an imaginative mind or whether his interests are of a literary nature. But one thing I know, as he is absorbed in watching the activities of these tiny creatures, he has forgotten this life we lead within these enclosures.

When the housewife has flicked the last speck of dust from her simple furnishings or has finished ironing her bundle of clothes, she carries her canvas chair outside her barrack door, and becomes enveloped in her knitting. Some ladies are crocheting rag rugs to throw on their cement floor.

The cupboards, chairs, tables, ironing boards, and such necessary conveniences are skillfully made by the men-folk. Materials are limited, in fact hard to find. Therefore apple boxes are broken and orange boxes are remodeled into dressing tables, and even couches. For such a rugged and simple life here in Camp, such home-made furnishings fit in harmoniously. The creator of each piece looks upon each finished product with a sense of pride. But when I realize that these bits of salvaged lumber are shaped into such pieces partly to while away the idle hours, I am overtaken with sadness. My sadness becomes more pronounced because this life we lead has no goal and this mode of living seems without promise of change. The Army determines our fate and we do not know how many years this pattern must continue.

In Japan there is a saying that goes "Living from day to day". Like wandering souls, who grope helplessly through the dark,

Our Corner, Tulare Assembly Center
by Shigeko Elizabeth Ozawa, July 31, 1942

we strive to grasp at the faintest light that comes in sight.
Even as the applause at the talent show did not sound whole-
hearted to my critical ears, so I believe that this feeling of
uncertainty is reflected in our many actions.

I returned to my barrack. The ground around it has been
carefully cultivated. The luxuriant green leaves of morning
glory, zinnias, green beans, and other vegetables greet my eye.
The morning glory vine has begun her climb upward along the
string that had been placed for her. It eventually will reach the
window to protect it from the strong rays of the sun.

In this Camp are former operators of large-scale farms.
They have brought an innate ability for growing vegetables and
flowers. Raising these products was their life. As much as they

yearn, they can no longer till the acreage they had in normal times. Though they desire to work throughout the day, to some, even this is restricted. Such is their fate. They plough a tiny plot beside their barrack. If they harvested this plot, it would most likely yield but a handful. Though they give it their loving attention each day, even this unharvested garden may have to be abandoned if orders come for our removal elsewhere. Nevertheless, these people continue to give these growing plants their consecrated care.

CHAPTER VII

M r. Miura of the Social Welfare Department very kindly invited me to Jimmie Sakoda's farewell party at 2:00 this afternoon in barrack C-20-1. Upon arriving there, I found over twenty young people from the Welfare Department and representatives of other Departments. The atmosphere was charged with conviviality. Miss Morooka was the mistress of ceremony. She is from Long Beach and is now working in the Welfare Department.

Mr. Miura opened the gathering with a word of farewell to Jimmie, who responded with warm words of appreciation. "The transfer permit for which I have waited so long has finally come. I should be happy and enthusiastic to leave, but since yesterday I have been overcome with despondency to think I must leave these friends I have learned to like."

James graduated this year from the University of California at Berkeley, where he majored in Psychology. He entered the Center determined to study the effect of such a congested form of living on the people. Because he wants to continue his sociological research, he is leaving for the Relocation Center at Tule Lake.

During our short acquaintance, everyone had grown fond of James, and though gaiety pervaded the room full of young people, there was also an undertone of regret over losing him. James had been a special help to me and I felt this regret deeply. Before evacuation, it was my dream to leave a perpetual record of life in this Center. About once in a thousand years, it is said that a catastrophe of such intensity occurs, that the heavens are disturbed and earth undergoes an upheaval. The contribution of Japanese over a period of fifty years toward building a better civilization on this coast was over-night turned into oblivion. I deeply felt my responsibility as an individual and as a Japanese to record this historical upheaval.

This urge to write surged from the depths of my soul and overcame my feelings of lack of ability as a writer. Mr. Miura continuously encouraged me. One day, as I sat in a quiet corner of his office bent over my writing, a voice beside me inquired, "What are you writing?" This was James.

"May I read some of it?" he asked. Of course I was glad, moreover I observed that he was pleased with what he had read. "This is so unusually interesting, won't you let me make an attempt at translating your writings?" he continued. His words struck me as a thunderbolt for I had not dreamed ever of having my evacuation diary translated into English.

"Will you translate my work for me? I do hope between the two of us, we can produce a good work." It was in such simple words and just as simple understanding that this writing in Tulare was launched. To have such an ideal young man help me with this work was more than I had hoped for. I had secretly hoped I could have him with me over an indefinite period of time. To lose him thus was a great personal loss.

The following Sunday afternoon at 2:00 o'clock he bade farewell to his many friends. As he shook my hand his last

Scene from East Side of Barracks, Tulare Assembly Center
by Shigeko Elizabeth Ozawa, July 30, 1942
(Note the low fence along this side of the Center).

words were, "We had just begun to feel our work. I regret leaving it undone." "Such unforeseen changes are only a part of life. You must study and make the best of your opportunities," was my reply. James had always impressed me as a serious, scholarly boy. I hope that he will be able to continue with his study and research.

A twenty-two year old boy attempted to leap the fence last night. He is now locked in a room in one of the buildings. Rumors whirled about this Camp all day. "My son has set such a terrible precedent, I cannot ask enough forgiveness of the people within this Center," were the words that came from his grieving mother. The father continued: "Such a disobedient boy should have been shot!" These parental laments were relayed to me by a friend of mine.

The penalty for violating rules and regulations of the Center are clearly written on large white billboards placed at regular intervals just within the fence. "Why must such unnecessary notices be posted, for surely no Japanese would break the rules of this Camp or attempt to jump the fence." Such were my thoughts when I first read this notice. But this happening has greatly disrupted my confidence in the Japanese ability to obey all orders implicitly.

A wave of anger shook me when I first heard the rumor. "Such a fool, can't he realize what the conditions are today?" The world over, regardless of race or creed, people are involved in a terrible material and spiritual struggle for which they are sacrificing their lives. This is no time for childish pranks or jokes. This is a time of absolute solemnity — serious and grave. For the sake of the rest of the Japanese, the severest punishment should be meted out to him, I thought. But as I continued to hear further details of this boy's life, my feeling subsided to one of sympathy. I suddenly wanted to talk to this youth who was locked in solitude, and console him.

I learned that he was a quiet youth who loved books and thinking. Just a few days before the outbreak of war, his parents noticed a sudden change come over their son. This forlorn child, what was it that caused him to change? What was it that caused him such inward suffering? If someone could have won his confidence — had been able to approach the working of his soul sooner, could have formed a heart-to-heart friendship — would he still have tried leaping over the fence?

The dreams that cause youthful blood to surge . . . when I wonder how long youth's restlessness can be curbed and quieted within these enclosures, I feel a wave of alarm pass over me. After breakfast hour, I see a line of youths lining the outer wall of the barracks. I cannot help but notice the aimless and far-off gaze in their eyes.

In order to escape the direct, merciless rays of the sun, groups of young men are gathered about in the protecting shade playing cards. These youths too impress me as having become spiritually lax. Then there are other types of less intelligent young people who, to while away the idle hours, are creating disturbing problems in our midst. I shudder as I think of the harmful influence such thoughtless leaders would have upon other innocent and straightforward brothers who surround them throughout the day.

A friend of mine, as a part of her work, called upon the family of one of these problem youths. This is what she discovered: Eight children and their parents living in one simple room. Ignorance, illiteracy, and indifference were expressed in the faces of both parents. "Since coming to this Center, my children have suddenly become possessed of evil-doing. Adults have taught them such manners," said one parent. "I could find no words with which to reply" was my friend's remark after her return from this visit.

With such undignified, ignorant, and uneducated parents, what example must they have set in sex conduct for their offspring within such cramped quarters. Such problems must be given serious thought.

The son of one of my friends is leaving this Center to attend a University. The joy that glowed upon his face as he left us has not yet left the curtain of my eyes. He had applied for a release permit, but it was slow in materializing. Hence, he was with us in camp for some time. He is scholarly — he is serious-minded. Education and learning was his life, interest, ambition, dream, and his love. The passion that possessed his life before evacuation gradually lost its ardor as his confinement continued. I began to notice a drop in his reading matter.

Movie magazines and such cheaper class of reading began to occupy his time.

The light of ambition that had shown in his eyes soon was replaced with a dull pessimistic shadow. To lie unshaven and outstretched on his cot gradually became a habit. Who could blame him? He could not help these circumstances, but his wife's, parents' and his friends' concern for him mounted each passing day.

Just as a climax, the permit for transfer finally came. The sudden miraculous reaction was like a doctor's injection to a dying patient. He cast aside his cheap magazine. With a burst of energy he was out of his bed. With surprising speed, he shaved his bearded face. He donned a clean suit. He sat erect before his desk. He picked up the dust-covered books. With maniacal fervor he was deep in his books again. His position was completely saved. As I think of the hundreds of youths and growing children from whom all opportunity was suddenly denied, just from having observed this one example, I can see now their inward sufferings.

They are occupied in all fields of work about the Center. Their time is consumed in other activities of entertainment, baseball and social life, but my heart feels the sorrow and anguish that vibrates from these youths. Their well of tears has ceased to flow naturally.

There are students of exceptional ability, whom people have praised. "Gentle and good natured" were the descriptions from their Caucasian instructors. To cruelly snap the unfolding bud and grind it 'neath their heels — no one has the right to do such a deed. This is war. How can we help it? This seems to be the only reason. If this were so, the responsibility lies upon no one. How can one ask youths to not cross the second

or third fence in order to leave this confinement? Until this war is over and peaceful days return, the vision of a tomorrow or the struggle for a fixed goal cannot be promised. I want them to abhor war! I want them to become builders and advocates for peace! Out of this cruel baptism, their only reward would be the experience that could not be expressed in words.

This morning the mother of the would-be escapist sat beside me at the breakfast table, with her white-haired, forlorn profile. Unaware of this mother's presence, a lively conversation regarding this boy was going on at the next table.

The mother stopped eating. She picked up her ears to listen to the irresponsible tongues that formed the conversation. "Lady, don't mind what people say of your son. His deed was not commendable but the thought that prompted the deed was not necessarily evil. You must learn to bear much and overlook the petty habits of people!" These were the only comforting words I could utter, and she tearfully replied: "This son who had been so respectful of people — to think that he should be the first to attempt such a deed." Why must people crucify this lovely old lady? With an oppressing loneliness, I left the mess-hall.

Today is Sunday. A thought came to me and I hastened to call my friend, Mrs. Ikami. The purpose was to visit this troubled lady. To the lady who sat so abjectly on her cot, we presented two bibles. One in Japanese for her to read, and another in English for her son who was temporarily imprisoned. If your spirit so desires, won't you come to our worship service tonight? With this invitation, we left her room. Because I firmly believed that such an invitation would comfort her, I made the best of the opportunity.

THE EVACUATION DIARY OF HATSUYE EGAMI

CHAPTER VIII

Lately a great number of men have returned from Montana, New Mexico and North Dakota to the various Assembly Centers. I stop to reflect on days that were indeed peaceful before the outbreak of war. I think of how the average Japanese family lived with hope for every possibility of progress in their future lives. One of the super-structures of Japanese progress, and contributions to Southern California in their fifty years' history here was embodied in "Lil Tokyo" in the heart of Los Angeles.

December 7th — that is one date that is carved deep into the heart and mind of every Japanese. The events of that fateful day caused this visible structure of Japanese progress to crumble before our eyes. Not only did we face economic catastrophe, but we were to be branded as enemies by the American public whom we had always loved. This quaint section of Los Angeles, described in songs and poetry, referred to as "Lil Tokyo" was overnight to become a ghost town.

In my opinion, it must be very hard for the younger generation, very few of whom have seen Japan, but who are typically American in action and in thought, to be looked upon by hateful and suspicious eyes. Fathers, and in many cases brothers, were sent away to internment camps. From that very moment, economic support for that family was threatened.

It wasn't so much the cold of winter nor the gloom cast over hearts by the rain or stormy skies. It was this unpredicted incident that caused us to live from second to second. The very sound of the winter gale and the sound of the rain that beat against our house seemed to bruise our souls and irritate our nerves.

Fortunately for me, my husband was not taken. But for the innumerable families, who overnight had been deprived of their fathers and husbands, I could not help but feel the deep shock, the mental, spiritual, and physical sufferings and anguish they experienced. I have never known the exact degree of their suffering, but I can fathom their experience to a certain extent.

Upon the actual return of their loved ones, that joy and relief must have been as deep and immeasurably great as the feeling when the fathers were taken from their homes. Many were the times I have seen husband and wife clasp each other's hands. No words were audible, for the wife with downcast face chokingly hid the tears that wet her cheeks. On the other hand, as I viewed these happy reunions, I could not help but notice one dejected, lonely figure.

Wait as she might, no notice of her husband's release has come. A person on the side could hardly fathom the anxiety of her waiting heart. So each time I view these reunions, my vision of these people in their lonely hours seems to grow in intensity.

CHAPTER VIII

I am reminded of that woman in her lonely hours. The vexing part of her experience is this: the morning that she was evacuated from Pasadena, her husband was returned to that city and sent on to Santa Anita. The train that bore her away from home had crossed paths with a train that brought her husband back. They are a childless couple. The husband is 82 and she is 64.

Because rumors reverberated about camp, she would walk the great distance to the gate each day. Each time on her way out to the gate her countenance was alight with expectation, but as she trudged back to her barrack, her form and face spoke of utter disappointment. These trips were countless. As those walks out to the gate continued, the change in her expression became less apparent, for whether she was going or returning, she was collected and reserved. This, to my mind, must be the result of deep resignation.

As the return of men from internment camps increased so these scenes of reunion increased. It became an ordeal for me to greet this lovely lady. Her long period of expectation brought to my mind a picture of a brave heart that was on the verge of collapsing after each disappointment. For me to even exchange casual words became an effort for I felt I could almost see the inner workings of her heart and soul. So I have kept my distance, and by so doing, I hoped to spare her any injury some of my words may cause. At present, my soul is brimming with a prayer that not only may her husband be returned, but that all the fathers and brothers return so that happiness might return to their respective families.

One day a lady was resting herself in a shady spot when a Japanese police officer approached her. "I'm sorry, madam, no one is permitted to loiter here." Just where the spot was, I do not know, but it must have been a prohibited place.

73

Scene from our door, Tulare Assembly Center
by Shigeko Elizabeth Ozawa, July 30, 1942 (A sign on the barracks
says "L7". Most of the people from Pasadena were in "L" section.
The Egamis were in L-8).

Nevertheless, that day was one of extreme heat. For a person who was accustomed to a milder climate, suddenly transplanted to where such heat waves prevail, it is only natural to seek every cool and shaded nook in this camp.

This frail woman, regardless of where she sought shelter from the penetrating heat, had found little relief. Just as she was recovering from the sharp words of this camp police, a Caucasian officer strolled upon the scene. He sized up the situation and with kind words assured the woman that she could stay where she was for on such a day, cool places were hard to find.

CHAPTER VIII

Yesterday, this incident occurred. Beyond the fence, there is a house around which grows a variety of flowers which are in bloom. In one corner of the yard is a clump of apricot trees. A slight breeze caused the glossy leaves to rustle and from among them, golden apricots seemed to peek.

Young men came out into this yard. One climbed the tree to pick the fruits, while the second held a bucket and the third stood by with his arm swathed in bandage. Opposite this spot, inside the fence, a crowd of innocent and roguish Japanese children gathered. In a carefree manner, they began to call out, "Give us some apricots. Give us some apricots!"

The youth with the bandaged arm began throwing apricots one by one across the fence. With great commotion, the youngsters gathered the fruits. As he threw again and again youth up to fifteen and sixteen gathered to receive the apricots. Apricots are thrown again. Again they are caught. Both the giver and the receiver glowed with smiles. From a distance, I could not help smile too as I watched. This scene was so beautiful in its innocence, tears came to my eyes.

Two or three days ago I heard another story. A five year old youngster tearfully begged that he be permitted to crawl between the barbed wires and run across the street to buy some candy. All the comforting words of his mother were to no avail. The sentry who stood outside the enclosure also became greatly distressed. To a child, reason means nothing. The sentry swooped upon the child and carried him across the street. No sooner had the sweets been purchased than he bore the bewildered child back across the street.

There was a child whose fancy was caught by a beautiful flower just across the enclosure. She craved this blossom. It is said that from infancy, this child had been possessed with a love for flowers. Likewise she tearfully begged her mother to get this flower. The following morning, an American neighbor who had witnessed this scene came to the fence with an armful of lovely blossoms.

Then this story has come to my ears. A tiny nursery school tot, seeing nothing but Japanese faces whirl about him each day thinks this Center is Japan. He implored his parents to take him back to America.

CHAPTER IX

JULY 4, 1942

For the past week, large write-ups have appeared in the Tulare News about the upcoming parade, the entertainments, and the meal for this festive day. On hearing the news, children clapped their chubby hands and cheered. Today's menu included fresh strawberries and watermelons. It brought joy to the hearts of children and grown-ups. The greatly anticipated July 4th arrived too soon.

On the morning of the fourth, my eldest daughter borrowed her youngest sister's dress and placed patches here and there on it. Donning the dress, she topped it with a wide-brimmed straw hat, such as worn by a farmer. Bewildered by the goings-on, I inquired and was told that Sachiko is entering the parade with her Club. I went to call for my friend Mrs. Sato to view the parade. At her quarters, I found a great commotion.

Miss Sato is the president of the girls' club. Besides being a capable leader, she is also a splendid entertainer. Today again, she had hit upon a rather unusual idea: she transformed herself into a Negro gentleman. Her face is painted black as ebony. On her lapel is a bright red flower. Her throat is encircled with an especially high collar. On her head is a high silk hat. Really, it is grand! I was told that this costume is an impersonation of Jack Benny's chauffeur, "Rochester".

Here at the Sato's living quarters are a number of girls attired in every conceivable costume. One has been completely transformed into an old, old lady, while another is a chorine (sic). "Rochester" and the young farmer's daughter Sachiko are strolling about amicably, arm in arm.

Mrs. Sato and I followed this strange mixture of costumes to the parade ground. People chuckled as this mottled group marched by. The costumed girls proceeded on to Evers Hall where the parade was to begin, while we went toward the grandstand. An incredible number of people gathered on the grandstand and on either side of the track. As there is yet time until the parade, we strolled toward the exhibit rooms.

In the first room we found knitting, embroidery, crocheting, applique, and tatting. Samples of beautiful handwork line the rooms. There is a huge blanket knit of wool yarn, sweaters for children and grown-ups. Then of finer thread are crochetted table-cloths, table-scarves, round pads for teapots and pillow cases. In the center of the room is an attractive screen, the result of patching an incredible number of scraps of wood. There is originality in it.

The next room contains *geta*, and general wood carvings. The *geta* is indispensable footwear for life in this camp. There are ever so many types of them lined on the table. Large and small, pretty ones, practical ones, and cute ones. Among them are some original creations, styles I have never seen before.

Another display consisted of ordinary stones that were painstakingly polished. There were ink-wells fashioned of several stones put together. These stone articles are the handiwork of men who have just returned from Montana. They must have hunted, polished, and created them in the several months of their internment.

There are many interesting carvings on bits of wood. They are the gifts brought back by men just returned from the internment camp in New Mexico. There are pictures, many beautiful drawings and between them are colorful artificial flowers. The next room is filled with written compositions, mathematics, sewing, and other school work.

Since there was limited time, we were only able to glance through this exhibit, but the thought that came to me: "Here in such a Center with limited facilities and material, it is amazing what a variety of creations were produced." In only three months' time, such an array of articles were made. Being a woman, and since I like needlework, the display of women's handwork especially impressed me. Women knitting intently in the shade! Knitting or sewing, whatever it be, what joys it produces even though on such a modest scale. Out of the whole universe, even on needle-point, we seek happiness. Is not this a woman's life?

The time for the parade is near. Mrs. Sato and I wait below the grandstand, where the chairman stands before the microphone. After the National Anthem and the flag salute, finally the 3/4 mile parade began. The Boy Scouts led, followed by Veterans of the last war. Mr. Aanonsen, manager of the Center and the other Caucasian administration staff joined the parade, lending a dignified air. The Fire Department, the Engineering Department, Sanitation, the Gardeners, Mess Halls, the Police Department, Girls' Clubs, Recreation

Department, Buddhist and Christian Sunday Schools, Social Welfare — each followed this solemn vanguard.

The creations and products of master minds in every conceivable branch have been responsible for the humorous, the colorful, and amusing groups that flowed in unending rhythm before our eyes.

The Police Department came with jail birds in their black striped attire. A ball and chain was attached to them so that the men staggered as they passed by. One finally came to an exhausted standstill and lay prostrate along the roadside. A stout Negress came with a dog. The dog is not genuine. It is a boy. As he crawls on all fours, he barks. Two boys are a donkey. At intervals excrement is dropped from its hind quarter. A boy follows with a dust pan and is busily engaged cleaning the droppings. What we thought was a waste-product, turns out to be fresh oranges.

As each unit passed, the spectators held their sides with laughter. Some have exhausted themselves so that they are resting on the ground. One cannot help smiling as the unassuming Sunday School youngsters march by.

The Queen, Yuriko Amemiya, appeared. With white gardenias on her head and on her bosom, with lovely roses in her hand, she nods and smiles pleasantly as she passes. She is a famous ballet dancer. Her character and ability are exceptional. She is indeed a lovable young lady, brilliant, yet unassuming. Above all, she loves people and in turn, she is loved by everyone.

Tulare News' unusual entry appears. At the end of this unit, Tetsu Komai, the veteran Hollywood character appears as an outlandish infant. As we laughed, cheered, and applauded his childish impersonation, we were equally impressed by the depth and reason for this caricature.

The parade ended. Since evacuation, this was the first Fourth of July. The end of the parade dropped the curtain on an amusing, entertaining morning. In this life of limited conveniences, the young people have contrived and created much out of the little they possessed.

Out of this life of stress, they still possess a suppliant attitude, and the ability to make room for a brilliant piece of humor. This revelation impressed me so, I was on the verge of tears. I was also greatly strengthened for having witnessed these things. In this war-torn world, to think that I was able to enjoy such a peaceful and enjoyable day filled me with a sense of deep gratitude.

THE EVACUATION DIARY OF HATSUYE EGAMI

CHAPTER X

JULY 5, 1942

Mr. Miura was to give a talk at the Buddhist service, so I went. I have wanted to hear him speak, but have never enjoyed the opportunity. "Why we must keep on Living," was the topic. I was born a Baptist, and was educated in a Baptist Mission School, so I had been denied an opportunity to familiarize myself with Buddhism.

Buddhism is a distinctly Oriental religion. Its philosophy is so deep it is fathomless. This religion is sedate, compared to progressive Christianity. It has a way of burrowing quietly rather than exposing itself boldly. I have observed it as a passerby and though I had wanted to study some of its precepts, I have never done so. Tonight, for the first time in my life, I am to attend a Buddhist service.

I selected a seat and settled myself with an anticipation throbbing within my breast. At 8:20 the service began. The format was very similar to that of a protestant service. This struck me as an unexpected disappointment.

While I was yet a child in Japan, I went to the temple enclosure. I recall the antiquated effect of a huge temple gate, the stone lanterns, the extremely high roof and then under the sweeping eaves, swarms of pigeons that caused an endless commotion as they came and went.

Pigeon, coo, coo
Coo, coo, as you fly to me;
Descend from the temple roofs,
I will give you beans;
So won't you eat it all,
Though you eat it,
Please don't fly away;
Coo coo as you play with me.

Any reference to Buddhist temples brings back to me those happy days I spent in the temple yard as I sang this children's song to the pigeons. I recall the fragrance of incense. As a naughty child, I tip-toed to the temple veranda just for a glimpse of the interior. The gold encrusted altar reposed there as solemnity itself.

My childish eyes saw fantastic mystery. I cannot forget the sound of a temple bell, its strange reverberation, and its lengthy echo. This sound drew me into a melancholy darkness. It would draw forth fond memories of my mother who had passed away. At times, the temple bell filled me with childish joy, but at other times it filled me with loneliness. That same Buddhism, what a change has come over it. What a light-giving religion it has become.

Just like our Christian Hymns, they have Buddhist hymns. Their hymns are far simpler and predominated by the minor key. The rosaries entwined about the wrists of those in the congregation seem to have changed but slightly. This

84

Buddhism — the temple — is so completely different from my past impressions. I feel an emptiness as though I had suddenly dropped something I had been holding. I was filled with fond memories of the resounding echoes of the temple bell. Mr. Miura's talk has finally begun.

Among the many questions that overwhelm us are the perplexing ones of "What is the meaning of life?" "Why must we go on living?" "What is the value of living?" "Why must we bear these sufferings in life?" These are some of the problems that bother us. Like the early philosophers, we, too, seek a solution to these questions.

Consider the animals that live in the wilds. An animal is totally ignorant of even a minute into its future. The animal has no way of determining when it might be caught in a stream of blood. Each moment, it exists on the borderline between life and death. If I were to be turned into an animal, I think I would prefer to die. Why does an animal live? It is given the instinct to live. It cannot help but live. Fortunately, nature breathes into everything the will to live. We of the human race are related to the animal. The fact that we possess a soul makes us differ. Possessing a soul has its assets as well as its drawbacks.

Occasionally, we become melancholy and begin to consider self-destruction. Instinct cries out for us to live, while our soul struggles back with a voice to destroy oneself. Within us is this discord between instinct and soul. Life's main aim is to consider from philosophic and psychological angles, how harmony can be created between instinct and mind. How can we proceed to bring harmony between these two elements within us?

Depending upon one's interpretation this may sound a bit difficult. But if the will to live has become one's set goal, then he is indeed a happy person because he has established harmony between his instinct and his mind. When a man becomes exposed to intense heat, he seems to feel that it is going to last forever; when we are overtaken by a storm, we feel that the storm is going to blow forever. When man meets death, is that the end of life?

Cool breezes are sure to bring relief to hot days; the sun is sure to follow storms. After illness, health is sure to follow. There are not only sorrows, but joys in this world. The smallest joy can make a man happy. I went from Chicago to Texas. Passing through the Ozarks in winter, I noticed a certain tree. It was exposed to wind and weather, leafless, lifeless, and desolate. Bleak and hopeless though it looked, when springtime came, the warm winds carried tidings of life. Bees would begin carrying pollen from distant blossoms to the buds that were opening on this tree. This tree is but a microscopic portion of nature.

Life is like an interwoven tapestry. Each of us is the strand and a part of the pattern. We are a part of it. Though we have sufferings, it does not mean that state must continue. Five thousand Japanese here in this Center are as one body. Each individual is a protoplasm within this body. The essence of philosophy is harmony and peace. Is not the conclusion the same?

I agreed with every bit of Mr. Miura's message.

So filled with faults, weaknesses, and spiritually poor as I am, I must focus my soul toward all high things, all lovely and pure things. With a humble soul I would earnestly strive to live. I would like to cling to this dream — to be perpetually young, perpetually child-like, forever sincere.

CHAPTER XI

JULY 9, 1942

Tonite is the very first commencement exercises, to be presided over by the Center manager, Mr. Aanonsen.

The stage is set directly below the grandstand in the vacant space. A special section of cap and gowned young people seat themselves just in front of this stage.

These graduates come from grammar schools, junior and senior high schools, junior colleges, and universities including the University of California at Davis, Santa Barbara State College, Compton Junior College, and Pacific College. Santa Maria, Ventura, Arroyo Grande, El Monte, Long Beach, Lompoc, Oxnard, San Marino, Santa Barbara, Santa Monica, and Venice are the junior and senior high schools represented here this evening.

Graduation Program

Chairman: . . . .*Nils Aanonsen*

Guests of Honor:
Officials of Tulare County Schools

Aria, from Suite Antique for two violins and piano
. . . .*Toshi Harada, Tsugio Iwohara, Kiyoko Oda*

Invocation . . . .*Rev. Susu-Mago*

Star Spangled Banner . . . .*Audience*

Introduction of Guests of Honor

Graduate Representatives:

"Education for Service" . . . .*Toshie Fujita*
High School Representative

"Education for Morale" . . . .*Amy Hiratzka*
Junior College Representative

"Education for Leadership" . . . .*George Takemoto*
College Representative

Praise be the Father . . . .*Gounod*
Choir directed by Ayako Matsumoto

Address . . . .*R. Nickel*
County Superintendent of Tulare Schools

Congratulatory message
Supervisor of Service Division

Processional March

Presentation of Graduates . . . .*Helen Osaka*

Granting of Diplomas . . . .*C.R. Carter*

Two Etudes by Chopin . . . .*John Fuyuume*

Special Awards . . . .*Nils Aanonsen*
California Scholarship Federation

America the Beautiful . . . .*Graduates*

Benediction . . . .*Rev. Susu-Mago*

Response . . . .*Choir*

88

The right wing is occupied by white-vested young people who are to furnish the choral music. Lately, there have been considerable improvements, but most things are yet in the makeshift state. Through the cooperative efforts of every young person participating, the setting has been made attractive. The heavy beams and posts at either side of the platform are concealed by a veil of refreshing green branches of trees. The stairs to be used by the graduates are bordered with daisy chains made by Mr. Tanaka's artificial flower class. On the stage is a lovely basket of artificial flowers.

The opening ceremonies of the commencement program finished and the graduates' speeches began. As each youthful voice flowed from the loudspeaker, I was deeply impressed at the seriousness of the speakers though I understood only in part. The sincerity with which they spoke worked like astringent upon my soul. I could not repress my tears.

In the past, at every graduation I have attended, some Japanese students participated. On the night of the event, parents, be they farmers or gardeners or business folk, attended these commencements with beating hearts. In conjunction with the graduation, a banquet of appreciation was given by Japanese of southern California to which principals and instructors of various schools were invited. This evening's graduates are all Japanese. The audience, too, is practically all Japanese. This fact strikes us as something out of the ordinary.

The graduates singing the anthem "America the Beautiful", carries me back to a similar formal affair last June in Pasadena. The Rose Bowl which holds 70,000 people was filled to capacity that night. Before dark, people began pouring into the Bowl. Youngsters wove in and out of the rows of seats selling popcorn and the night's programs. The faces of people were lighted with a certain, wholesome glow. The very atmosphere itself was charged with a suppressed sort of joy.

All the graduates from junior high schools through nursing school graduates had assembled. That night 1500 youths were to be graduated. The junior high graduates were in white, high school graduates in pink, and junior college graduates in caps and gowns. This colorful stream moved silently toward the grandstand. The Pasadena Junior College Band played the Processional. The theme for the year's commencement was: religion, education, and music.

The white, hot sun dipped from view. With the lengthening shadows the heat gradually dispelled. As night enveloped the Bowl, varicolored beams wove and interwove across the arena. In this sea of moving lights, the 70,000 humans sat in solemnity almost riveted to their seats.

In such a grand setting, a youth by the name of Tanaka gave the graduation oration. According to Dr. Harbeson's explanation, he had averaged a grade of 99% from junior high to junior college winning an envious record never known before in the history of Pasadena Junior College. This youth's voice came flowing from the loudspeaker. The rustling in the audience hushed, the instant they heard his voice. I have forgotten the context of this commencement speech, but the atmosphere and the response of the audience to this oration lingers with me as an undying memory.

Tonight's commencement here in the Center is leaving a far deeper impression and significance. I am not the only one who is thus impressed. I know that all the others hold a common thought. At the same instant, I wondered what these graduates are planning to do — what is to become of them. As in *Quo Vadis*, the meaning of the title itself leaves a dark cloud hanging over us. But I am also thinking of a letter I received from a youth who had left the Center to study in an eastern college.

"Coming here, my dreams and the actual realities are so completely different, I am greatly surprised. Everything in general is so expensive, I don't know just how to tell you. Sugar scarcity is to be expected. Fresh vegetables are so dear; they seldom reach our mouths. Gas is being rationed, as you know, and we cannot shave ourselves regularly for want of hot water. While I was in the Center, hot and cold water were available all hours of the day and night. Showers were accessible at all times. Under these circumstances, I am beginning to envy those of you who are in the various Centers.

"Since coming out into this area of freedom, I have discovered that it is not only the Japanese who cannot study. I have discovered that the Caucasians students too, are putting up with sacrifices. Many are dropping out of school due to unknown difficulties. Many are called to the armed forces, while others discontinue their education to aid their country by working in various defense industries. The Japanese students, under these circumstances, are not justified in demanding continuation of their education.

"We must remind ourselves that these are abnormal times. If a youth loved acquiring knowledge so much, he should be able to study under any circumstance, under any handicap. Although the students are in the Centers, they are yet able to ask for necessary material by mail. On the other hand, an aspiring youth can seek out someone who is well versed in the field he wishes to study. To think that study cannot be done outside of school is a grave mistake."

"Whither goest thou, Quo Vadis?" refers not only to Japanese, but to the whole human race. It not this a problem the world over? What is the sole aim of education? In this regard, I have pondered deeply, but this problem seems too

great and far too difficult. There is, however, one point which
I think I understand, That is the mystery of the creation of the
universe and the mystery that shrouds the limitless spaces. The
wonders of the chemical world, the immeasurable greatness of
the artistic world. There is one great revelation I know is present in all of these different fields. That is the love of God. In
all the known world, man claims to be the master and claims
the highest rank of all living things. If man were to delve and
search into the mysteries of the Creator's works, he must do so
in all sincerity and humility. Does not man owe this endeavor
to his God? This, I think, is the core and the essence of the
search for knowledge.

In his book, "Unity in the Arts" Wagner asserts: All art
reverts back to music, and doing so, they are unified. Poetry,
painting, drama, and sculpturing — these are entwined into
music and become a musical drama. Being thus transfigured,
art attains the highest elevation.

Dr. Millikan of Caltech in Pasadena said, "Many of you
are studying here because you happen to be outstanding in
zoology, chemistry, or engineering. To send such students out
into the world prepared only in these specialized fields does not
mean that the school has fulfilled its duty as an educational
institution. You who enter the world as social beings will discover that the coming age is an age of complications. You must
adjust yourself to the needs of this age. You must analyze
earnestly, maintaining a straightforward perspective with
knowledge that is fitting to the standard of that time. You
must exert every creative power to present these spiritual quali-
ties and offer your knowledge as a sacrifice truly fitting to
mankind.

"In four consecutive years, I have endeavored to teach you to serve mankind. This effort is the result of my convictions. The historic background of men and their efforts for progress must be ever present in your conscience. A deep understanding is the greatest prerequisite to students of science."

The great Wagner expressed the need for understanding and unity. The great scientist Millikan, expressed the same thought using science as a medium. Is not this similarity in thought interesting? Wagner argued that music should be placed in the highest ranks. The scientist pleads with his students to exert their endeavors so that science might be placed in the highest position. I would plead that all man's efforts should be returned to our Creator as a perfect sacrifice upon God's altar.

If we placed God in the center of all men's efforts and recognize God as occupying the highest position known in our universe, only then can man's educational value rise as he strives for progress. Man's spiritual well-being, enlightenment, and general progress — do they not become apparent after he has recognized the divinity of his Creator?

Though fences surround us, the air continues to circulate, the songs of birds are carried to us. The trees are green; white clouds drift dreamily overhead. Let us be gentle. Let us be thankful. Let us love everybody. Let us try to find intimacy with our Creator and strive for higher planes of endeavor.

THE EVACUATION DIARY OF HATSUYE EGAMI

CHAPTER XII

JULY 13, 1942

Today is my birthday, and my last child, George's birthday also. Twelve years ago today, having had three girls until then, I was fearful of another girl being added to the family. Instead, a ten pound baby boy arrived with bouncing energy. That day was Sunday, it was also extremely hot. Since it was my birthday, my children were in the midst of preparing a chicken dinner. And as a present, George was born to us.

My children and I had been planning to invite our immediate barrack neighbors to all of our birthday celebrations, but two or three days ago, due to a sudden unfortunate occurrence, I fell into the throes of depression and have been left with a feeling of utter vacancy. This persistent unhappiness has haunted me like an apparition day and night and not unlike an invalid or an imbecile, I have hung my head. It is not my wish to write of this happening. It would rather bury it in forgetfulness.

Having compared life to the fragrance of a flower, the song of birds on the wing, and all the heavenly virtues, was my great mistake. I gave no consideration for what evils lay hidden in the heart of some individual, but I took for granted that everyone was in a like frame of mind and without exception would welcome me.

I am in the midst of a conflict. I want to dislike, to hate, to hold a grievance against a person. The unpleasantness of the occurrence is not the cause of my suffering. Instead, it is the conflict of thoughts within me that causes me such agony.

I have read in someone's writing: "hate is an element that can be forgotten with the passing of time." That indeed is true. Love is an element that remains. Despite the passing of time, love raises its head, increases and expands, becoming a part of a beautiful soul. Is this not one of the beauties to be revealed in man?

My birthday was a total failure. Rather than having such a festive occasion, I am drawing the strength from my friends as they comfort me.

Around ten o'clock in the morning in a spell of loneliness, I walked aimlessly out toward the grandstand. Near the administration building, Mr. Miura approached me with his usual broad smile. "Mr. Aanonsen wants to see you, so won't you see him?" he asked.

I was overwhelmed with joy but in this state of mind and being in a soiled dress, I pleaded, "Please, can't you arrange it some other time? I must change my dress." I strained to calm the excitement that pounded within my breast, thinking that as I washed my face and dressed myself, I would be able to retrieve a little of the brightness that had so deserted me. But Mr. Miura, unable to perceive the condition of my mind, insisted, and without further delay, hurried to the office to call Amy Morooka, who was to accompany me to the interview.

CHAPTER XII – JULY 13, 1942

Amy and I found our way to Mr. Aanonsen's office which was light and peacefully quiet. A large mahogany desk was placed diagonally in one corner of this room. As we entered, Mr. Aanonsen arose from his seat, "I am so glad to have the privilege of meeting you," he said as he extended his hand to shake mine. Amy and I seated ourselves on the chairs that were placed opposite Mr. Aanonsen. There, for some time, a quiet conversation ensued.

The fact that Mr. Aanonsen had been reading my humble writing had been communicated to me through Mr. Miura, but today, Mr. Aanonsen himself encouraged me. Two weeks ago, while it was still early in the morning, and my being a sleepy-head, I was still in bed when Mr. Miura, in his energetic way, glowing with his usual smile, came to tell me, "Mr. Aanonsen has told me that your writing is interesting so you must continue to write with all your might."

I cannot express fully the importance of these words of encouragement. Little sorrows, and little joys are a great influence to a writer or an artist. These elements are necessary to our lives. Mr. Aanonsen's encouragements were great enough, but Mr. Miura's visit so early in the morning, bearing these kind words from Mr. Aanonsen, and the earnestness of his desire to strengthen me, impressed me deeply.

My enthusiasm is fading. I must brace myself, I remind myself; but Mr. Miura seems to sense the slightest change that comes over me. At every possible opportunity he encourages and strengthens me. This morning especially, I was in the depth of depression and was sad. I could not write a line. My soul was on the verge of wringing itself shut — of becoming withered and lifeless, but immediately following Mr. Miura's visit, this soul of mine took life again.

Write — I must write more and more. I must observe all matters with a warm heart. I must fix my focus straight-forward. My soul was filled again with light, my bosom swelled with a greater hope — it was my desire to nurture this feeling. My birthday party was a failure, but the resurrection of hope within me brought back the deep significance of that day.

Mr. Arima who cooks in the "C" kitchen, along with his wife, has been my friend for many years. The day following July 4th, Mr. Arima said: "Mr. Aanonsen is indeed a wonderful person. To have such a man as manager of the Center; we must consider ourselves fortunate. Cooking is indeed such hard work, occasionally, one is tempted to resign, but if it were to serve such a man as Mr. Aanonsen, I could undergo any hardship."

I asked him the reason for this sudden outburst, and he replied: "The afternoon of July 3rd, I received a burn. As I stood over the stove, frying the meat for supper, another cook stood beside me doing likewise. As he transferred the searing meat to another container, it slipped and fell, enveloping the fingers of my hand. I ran to the hospital. There as the attending physician strove to extricate the clinging meat from my hand, all the skin underneath the meat came off in the process. The pain caused me no end of suffering."

Surely, Mr. Arima was entitled to a good rest. Instead, because he felt his responsibility, he continued with his work. At this point, I should like to offer my fullest respect and gratitude to the cooks of this Center. Of all the work in this Center, I believe none is quite as busy as that of the cooks. The heat produced from the coal is said to reach 400 degrees. In the midst of midsummer, they work silently exposed to this suffocating atmosphere, yet their salary is exactly the same as that of other workers. Simply because they must feed the people, they are susceptible to an endless number of complaints. If these cooks did not possess this sense of service, it would so easy for them to resign.

The July Fourth which children and grown-ups had anticipated was one of the busiest days for the cooks. Ninety chickens were distributed to each kitchen. Kind Mr. Arima had smilingly told me his desire to make the menu for the Fourth as tasty as he could. He wished to satisfy everyone if it were possible.

In the morning was the parade. "C" kitchen was to enter. It had been among the first in this Center to receive an award for the finest reputation. Enthusiastically, Mr. Arima told me he would go out to join the parade. With one arm trussed in a bandage and a bread board in the other, he marched. No sooner had he reached the end of the parade, but he veritably ran back to his kitchen. Ninety chickens were awaiting his attention. Almost forgetful of his pains, he continued his conscientious service.

The feast for the evening was prepared, so Mr. Arima stepped outside for a rest when suddenly Mr. Aanonsen came into view. As he saw the injured cook, he inquired in a warm and kindly tone, "I hear you've sustained a severe burn. Does it still hurt you? Are you sure you do not need to rest?" "It hurts me a bit, but we have cooked ninety chickens in this kitchen. We have tried preparing them so that everyone will enjoy them. That is why I have worked. Everyone is eating now, so I am out here resting."

Mr. Aanonsen thanked Mr. Arima for this explanation and asked, "Could I have a glimpse of the people who are now enjoying their dinner?" "Please" he replied. So Mr. Aanonsen stepped inside the mess hall, and with a smile of satisfaction lighting his face, stood and watched the faces that filled the hall.

"Mr. Aanonsen is indeed a man with a warm heart" continued Mr. Arima. If he were to the contrary, an indifferent individual, he could easily have sent someone in his stead, but the fact that he is such a considerate man, he wanted to see for himself. When he inquired of my condition, I forgot all the suffering and the pain in my hand." I am sure that similar stories exist throughout this Center.

As soon as I arrived in the Center, I was introduced to Mr. Aanonsen. At various times since then, I have seen him as he walked about, or as he stood on the stage to preside or make an announcement during some program. But at the time of the interview, as I spoke to him, I was deeply impressed. He is quiet. He is reserved. People say he is a thinker. Like a spiritual person or an artist, he strives to satisfy people. There is not the slightest trace of a sharp diplomat, nor a thick-blooded, influential businessman in him. There is warmth, there is quiet. The depth in his eyes convey beauty, righteousness and all the virtues. They shine with wisdom and intelligence. The fact that Mr. Aanonsen is reserved in his ways, only seems to attract the respect of people.

We, 5,000 in this Center must consider ourselves exceedingly fortunate to have been blessed with such a director. According to Mr. Miura, Mr. Aanonsen is not a native of this country, but of Norway. Despite being a foreigner, he is thoroughly Americanized. The fact that he was trusted and appointed manager of such a community deserves to be written of with a 'special pen'. That Japanese were denied citizenship is a deplorable fact, but before we continue lamenting this denial, we must ask ourselves this question. Have we made a special effort to Americanize ourselves? I feel we have not expended the energy to Americanize ourselves.

What can be said of one who finds himself a stranger in a strange household — a dependent — forever boasting of his home in Japan — pining and yearning for it. If he gives no respect for the atmosphere of this strange household, if he has responded little or exerted little effort to add harmony to this atmosphere, he has been ill-mannered, unreasonable and extremely willful.

Someone who sincerely desires to become a citizen of the United States — before he could claim that right, must exert an earnest endeavor to develop an attitude of humility and faith toward acquiring this privilege. If this privilege is denied, I think it means that he did not exert his sincerest effort.

By the end of August 1942, the residents of Tulare Assembly Center had been moved to Gila River, Arizona where most of them spent the remaining war years.

ADDITIONAL RESOURCES

For an extensive bibliography on the evacuation and internment of Japanese Americans during the Second World War, a
good source is **The Lost Years, 1942-46**, by the Manzanar
Committee, Los Angeles. It is available from them at 1566
Curran Street, Los Angeles, CA 90026.

Other publications which I have found helpful to my understanding include:

Edmiston, James, **Home Again**, New York: Doubleday and Co.,
1955.
    *A fictional account of three generations of Japanese Americans
in Northern California, including their internment experience, written by a sympathetic Caucasian who assisted with relocation. This
book is especially appropriate for middle and high school students.*

Kessler, Lauren, **Stubborn Twig: Three Generations in the
Life of a Japanese American Family**, New York, Random
House, 1993.
    *The Yasui family of Hood River, Oregon, is profiled through
their immigrant, agricultural, internment, and post-internment expe-
riences. Especially significant is Min Yasui's legal challenge to
Executive Order 9066.*

Kikumura, Akemi, **Through Harsh Winters: The Life of a
Japanese Immigrant Woman**, Novato, CA: Chandler and
Sharp Publishers, 1981.
    *Akemi Kikumura tells the story of her mother and her adjust-
ments to life in America. Although the setting is rural, there are
similarities with Mrs. Egami.*

Kikumura, Akemi, **Promises Kept: The Life of an Issei Man**,
Novato, CA: Chandler and Sharp Publishers, 1991.
    This is the story of Akemi Kikumura's father.

Kikuchi, Charles, *The Kikuchi Diary: Chronicle from an American Concentration Camp*, Champaign, University of Illinois Press, 1973.

   Like Mrs. Egami's diary, Kikuchi's covers the initial impact of the Assembly Center, in his case Tanforan, a race track in the San Francisco bay area.

Kogawa, Joy, *Obasan*, Boston: David R. Godine, 1981.

   Japanese Canadians were also subjected to dislocation, incarceration, racism, and hardship. This novel conveys a sense of the Japanese Canadian experience.